Understanding

Roman Catholicism

Rick Jones

CHICK PUBLICATIONS

For a complete list of distributors nearest you call us at (909) 987-0771 or visit us on the world wide web at www.chick.com

CHICK PUBLICATIONS

P. O. Box 3500, Ontario, Calif. 91761-1019 USA
Tel: (909) 987-0771 • Fax: (909) 941-8128
www.chick.com
Email: postmaster@chick.com

Printed in the United States of America

© 1995 by Rick Jones
rjones@chick.com

ISBN: 0-937958-48-4
Library of Congress Card Catalog Number: 95-092609

Preface

As a child growing up in a Roman Catholic home, I often wondered about the practices of the Catholic church. One example is "eating meat on Fridays." During my childhood years, this was a sin that would send you to hell. Then one day the church declared that it was now okay. Questions popped into my young mind like: "Did God change His mind?" "If so, why?" I asked myself, "Why was it sinful to eat meat on Fridays, but not on any other day?" I wondered, "How did God in heaven get word down to man that this practice no longer bothered Him?" I thought about the millions of people who had died and gone to hell for committing this sin, and asked myself: "Now that it's no longer a sin, will God release them from hell and bring them to heaven and apologize?"

Let me ask you... do you have questions about what your church teaches? If so, this book can help. Keep in mind, someday you will stand before God, and you won't be able to say, "See my priest... he takes care of my spiritual matters." You will give an account of your own life.

That's why this book is so important. Using plain, easy-to-understand language, it will answer those nagging questions that have bothered you for so long. With your eternal destiny at stake, nothing is more crucial.

May God richly bless you.

Contents

"That the God of our Lord Jesus Christ, the Father of glory, may give unto you the spirit of wisdom and revelation in the knowledge of him: The eyes of your understanding being enlightened..."

Ephesians 1:17-18

Introduction

In recent years, there has been a merging of Roman Catholicism with traditional Protestantism. Many on both sides now claim those in the other camp as their Christian brothers and sisters. This was unheard of several years ago, but today:

- Roman Catholic clergy appear regularly on Christian television, promoting unity between Catholics and Protestants.
- Christian radio stations broadcast Roman Catholic programs.
- Christian bookstores carry a variety of material appealing to Roman Catholics.

Have the two sides, in fact, merged? Are they both now preaching the same message? Do both hold the same cardinal doctrines?

To discover the answer to these questions, I began an exhaustive study of the 1994 *Catechism of the Catholic Church*. Using this particular Catechism was important for two reasons:

1. This catechism is the ***official*** source for all Roman Catholic doctrine. No one can deny that it contains the actual teachings of the Roman Catholic church.

2. Published in 1994, this is the first new catechism in over 400 years. Therefore you can be assured that you are reading the current teachings of the Roman Catholic church, not what it may have taught three hundred years ago.

In this book, we will examine 37 of the most critical Roman Catholic doctrines, then let the facts speak for themselves.

You will not find personal opinions or philosophies presented here. This is strictly a declaration of true Roman Catholic doctrine and how those doctrines compare with the Bible. You must draw your own conclusions and make your own decisions.

Neither is this a book of judgment or condemnation. It's sole purpose is to help you better understand Catholic doctrine so you will be prepared when you stand before God for judgment, as we all must do after death:

> "And as it is appointed unto men once to
> die, but after this *the judgment:*"
>
> Hebrews 9:27

My heart breaks at the thought of anyone hearing
Jesus proclaim the following words to them on that
day:

> "I never knew you: depart from me, ye
> that work iniquity." Matthew 7:23

Yet the Bible reveals that the Lord will proclaim those
very words to many *religious* people. Knowing this, it
is vital that you not blindly follow anyone. Learn these
Roman Catholic doctrines for yourself so you will be
able to face God with confidence.

As you read, my sincere prayer is that God will reveal
His truth to your heart and mind. God bless you.

Who is The Final Authority?

Before we begin our examination of specific Roman Catholic doctrines, we must determine who will be the final authority.

Here we encounter our first major discrepancy. The Bible maintains that *it* is the one and only final authority, while Catholicism teaches that three final authorities exist. The 1994 *Catechism of the Catholic Church* declares:

> "It is clear therefore that, in the supremely wise arrangement of God, sacred Tradition, Sacred Scripture, and the Magisterium of the Church are so connected and associated that one of them cannot stand without the others. Working together, each in its own way, under the action of the one Holy Spirit, they all contribute effectively to the salvation of souls." (Pg. 29, #95)

According to this passage, the Scriptures, church tradition (teachings handed down through the ages), and the Magisterium (the task of giving an authentic interpretation of the Word of God) are all equal in importance. (See also Pg. 25, #82.)

According to Catholic doctrine, church tradition and the magisterium are just as much the Word of God as are the written Scriptures:

> "Sacred Scripture is the speech of God as it is put down in writing under the breath of the Holy Spirit. And (Holy) Tradition transmits in its entirety the Word of God which has been entrusted to the apostles by Christ the Lord and the Holy Spirit." (Pg. 26, #81)

The obvious question is, what happens when these three "final authorities" disagree with each other? The Catechism gives this answer:

> "The task of giving an authentic interpretation of the Word of God, whether in its written form or in the form of Tradition, has been entrusted to the living, teaching office of the Church alone. This means that the task of interpretation has been entrusted to the bishops in communion with the successor of Peter, the Bishop of Rome." (Pg. 27, #85)

It is important to note that when the Catechism explains that the task of interpreting the Word of

God was entrusted to the "Church," it is referring exclusively to the Roman Catholic church. Such is the case throughout the Catechism. "The Church" always refers to the Roman Catholic church.

The Catechism repeats the same doctrine using different words:

> "For, of course, all that has been said about the manner of interpreting Scripture is ultimately subject to the judgment of the Church which exercises the divinely conferred commission and ministry of watching over and interpreting the Word of God." (Pg. 34, #119)

Therefore, the Catechism concludes that the one final authority is not the Bible, but the current teaching of the Catholic church, since she is the only one qualified to provide an "authentic interpretation" of God's Word.

Does the Bible agree?

If the Bible, tradition and the teachings of the Catholic church are all, in fact, the Word of God, then the Bible will concur with this teaching. Unfortunately for Catholicism, it does not. In fact, quite the contrary is true. God declares in the Bible that His written Word always has been, and always will be—perfect:

"Thy word is true from the beginning: and every one of thy righteous judgments *endureth for ever.*"

Psalm 119: 160

"The words of the Lord are pure words: as silver tried in a furnace of earth, purified seven times. Thou shalt keep them, O Lord, thou shalt *preserve them from this generation for ever.*"

Psalm 12:6-7

The Bible boldly declares that *it* is the *only* final authority:

"Sanctify them through thy truth: *thy word is truth.*"   John 17:17

In the book of Revelation, God delivers this blistering warning about tampering with His written Word:

"For I testify unto every man that heareth the words of the prophecy of this book, If any man shall *add unto these things,* God shall add unto him the plagues that are written in this book: And if any man shall *take away from the words of the book* of this prophecy, God shall take away his part out of the book of life, and out of

> the holy city, and from the things
> which are written in this book."
>
> Revelation 22:18-19

The Apostle Paul advises Bible readers how they
should react to those who teach doctrines contrary to God's written Word:

> "Now I beseech you, brethren, mark
> them which cause divisions and offen-
> ces **contrary to the doctrine which ye
> have learned;** and avoid them. For
> they that are such serve not our Lord
> Jesus Christ, but their own belly; and
> by good words and fair speeches
> deceive the hearts of the simple."
>
> Romans 16:17-18

Paul admonishes true believers to avoid **anyone**
who teaches doctrines contrary to the written
Scriptures. He also reveals the consequences of
believing such false teachings:

> "But though we, or an angel from
> heaven, preach **any** other gospel unto
> you than that which we have preached
> unto you, **let him be accursed.**"
>
> Galatians 1:8

Then Paul immediately repeats himself:

> "As we said before, so say I now again,
> If any man preach *any* other gospel
> unto you than that ye have received,
> *let him be accursed.*"   Galatians 1:9

Thus, when Catholic doctrine contradicts God's written Word, those who side against the Holy Scriptures will be "accursed."

The writer of Proverbs delivers the same stern warning to anyone who would dare change the written Word of God:

> "Every word of God is pure: he is a
> shield unto them that put their trust
> in him. *Add thou not unto his
> words,* lest he reprove thee, and thou
> be found a liar."   Proverbs 30:5-6

God's Word is settled forever

God pronounces that His Word was written once and has been forever settled:

> *"For ever,* O Lord, thy word is settled
> in heaven."   Psalm 119:89

> "But the word of the Lord endureth
> *for ever..."*   1 Peter 1:25

> "... the word of our God shall stand
> *for ever."*   Isaiah 40:8

> "Being born again, not of corruptible seed, but of incorruptible, by the word of God, which liveth and abideth *for ever.*"   1 Peter 1:23

God's Word is perfect

God's Word can't change because it's perfect just the way it is:

> "The law of the LORD is *perfect,* converting the soul…"   Psalm 19:7

Catholicism claims that only the leadership of the Catholic church can properly interpret the written Word, but the Bible disagrees:

> *"… no prophecy of the scripture is of any private interpretation.* For the prophecy came not in old time by the will of man: but holy men of God spake as they were moved by the Holy Ghost."   2 Peter 1:21

Where does God want people to obtain their doctrine… from a priest—or from the Bible?

> "All *scripture* is given by inspiration of God, and is profitable for doctrine, for reproof, for correction, for instruction in righteousness:"
> 2 Timothy 3:16

Paul is not alluding to the magisterium or church tradition here because the previous verse reads:

> "And that from a child thou hast known the holy scriptures, which are able to make thee wise unto salvation through faith which is in Christ Jesus."   2 Timothy 3:15

Since the Catholic church was not yet in existence when Paul penned these words, he could not have been referring to the teachings of Catholicism.

Did God give away His authority?

As these and hundreds of other scripture verses make plain, God never gave anyone the authority to add to or change His Word. It's perfect and complete, just as He wrote it.

One of the first questions you must answer for yourself is, "Did God violate all these Scriptures by giving the pope and the Catholic church the right to change His Word, though He said He never would?"

The Pharisees

While Jesus walked the earth, He publicly rebuked the Pharisees, the religious leaders of his day:

> "Howbeit in vain do they worship me,

> teaching for doctrines the command-
> ments of men. For laying aside the
> commandment of God, ye hold the
> tradition of men..."   Mark 7:7-8

Jesus was upset that the Pharisees had elevated their tradition above God's Word because He knows that the Word of God leads people to eternal life, while the traditions of men lead people to eternal destruction.

Though these religious leaders obeyed all the rules of their religion, look what Jesus said awaited them:

> "Ye serpents, ye generation of vipers,
> how can ye escape the ***damnation of
> hell?***"   Matthew 23:33

When the Pharisees asked Jesus why His disciples transgressed the traditions of the elders, Jesus answered them with a question of His own:

> "Why do ye also transgress the com-
> mandment of God by your tradition?"
>   Matthew 15:3

Jesus always elevated the Scriptures above traditions:

> "Jesus answered and said unto them,
> Ye do err, not knowing ***the scriptures,***

nor the power of God."

Matthew 22:29

God's unchanging Word has always been the final authority, never the traditions of men:

> "Beware lest any man spoil you through philosophy and vain deceit, *after the tradition of men,* after the rudiments of the world, *and not after Christ."* Colossians 2:8

Christians in New Testament times knew what the final authority was:

> "These were more noble than those in Thessalonica, in that they received the word with all readiness of mind, and *searched the scriptures daily,* whether those things were so." Acts 17:11

To determine if what they had heard was true, these people went to the final authority, the written Scriptures. Jesus says of His Words:

> "… If a man love me, he will keep *my words:* and my Father will love him, and we will come unto him, and make our abode with him. *He that loveth me not keepeth not my sayings…"* John 14:23-24

Consider these words from the Apostle Paul:

> "For this cause also thank we God
> without ceasing, because, when ye
> received the word of God which ye
> heard of us, ye received it not as the
> word of men, but as it is in truth, ***the
> word of God...***" 1 Thessalonians 2:13

When Paul preached the Word of God to these people, it was not Catholic doctrine because Catholicism didn't exist yet.

Conclusion

God doesn't change (Malachi 3:6) because He is perfect. His Son, Jesus, doesn't change (Hebrews 13:8) because He is perfect. Why, then, should God's perfect Word keep changing?

As you read the remainder of this book, you will be forced to decide which you believe is the final authority: God's written Word, or the teachings and traditions of the Catholic church.

Your decision will become critical as you discover that God's Word and the teachings of Catholicism are diametrically opposed on every doctrine we will examine.

Will you side with the words of God or the traditions of men?

"Heaven and earth shall pass away,
but *my words* shall not pass away."
Matthew 24:35

Note: Since the written Scriptures plainly state that they alone are the Word of God, for the remainder of this book, all references to the Word of God or God's Word will refer to the written Scriptures only, not the traditions of the Catholic church or the magisterium.

"… let God be true, but every man a liar…" Romans 3:4

1

Salvation Through The Church

Roman Catholicism teaches that salvation is available only through the Catholic church:

> "The Second Vatican Council's Decree on Ecumenism explains: 'For it is through Christ's Catholic Church alone, which is the universal help toward salvation, that the fullness of the means of salvation can be obtained.'" Pg. 215, #816

Here, the 1994 catechism reaffirms the existing teaching of Vatican II, that salvation can be obtained **only** through the Roman Catholic church. The catechism leaves no doubt that the Catholic church is necessary for salvation:

> "...all salvation comes from Christ the Head through the Church which is his Body: Basing itself on Scripture and Tradition, the Council teaches that the Church, a pilgrim now on earth, is necessary for salvation..." Pg. 224, #846

Past popes have taught this doctrine, as have previous catechisms and church fathers. Here is but one example...

On May 7, 2001, Pope John Paul II told 2,000 youth gathered at the Greek-Melkite Cathedral of Damascus that "you cannot be a Christian if you reject the Church founded on Jesus Christ."[1]

Catholic friend, you personally may not believe this, but your pope does. And it is an official doctrine of your religion.

If you check God's Word on this subject, you will not find a single verse requiring one to go through a church to be saved. In fact, the opposite is taught:

> "For whosoever shall *call upon the name of the Lord* shall be saved."
>
>   Romans 10:13

When Jesus died on the cross, He paid the full price for the sins of all mankind. According to God's Word, anyone can go directly to Him for salvation. Jesus Himself announced that:

[1]From article *"Pope Meets with Youth of Various Christian Confessions,"* Vatican City, 5/7/01 (VIS) reported by the Catholic Information Network, 5/9/01, N.86

> "He that **believeth on the Son** hath everlasting life: and he that believeth not the Son shall not see life; but the wrath of God abideth on him."
>
> John 3:36

Jesus preached:

> "He that heareth my word, and **believeth on him that sent me,** hath everlasting life…" John 5:24

> "He that believeth on me **hath everlasting life.**" John 6:47

Jesus repeats this message in John 3:16, 3:18, and 6:40. If the Catholic church really is necessary for salvation, then Jesus Christ is a liar.

The Apostle Paul gives step by step instructions on how to be saved:

> "That if thou shalt confess with thy mouth the Lord Jesus, and shalt **believe in thine heart** that God hath raised him from the dead, thou shalt be saved. For with the heart man **believeth** unto righteousness; and with the mouth confession is made unto salvation." Romans 10:9-10

Notice, no church is required. So if Catholicism is

right, then the Apostle Paul is also a liar. And since he wrote under the inspiration of the Holy Spirit, the Holy Spirit is a liar as well.

The Apostle John teaches:

> "But as many as received (trusted in) him, to them gave he power to become the sons of God, even to them that ***believe on his name.***" John 1:12

John says you become God's child by believing in Jesus Christ. If this Catholic doctrine is true, then John's name must be added to the list of liars.

But John is not a liar. Jesus never requires a church for salvation:

> "To him (Jesus) give all the prophets witness, that through his name ***whosoever believeth in him shall receive remission of sins.***" Acts 10:43

The key is belief in Christ, not a church:

> "For I am not ashamed of the gospel of Christ: for it is the power of God unto salvation ***to every one that believeth...***" Romans 1:16

According to Paul, Timothy needed faith in Christ to be saved, not a church:

"And that from a child thou hast
known the holy scriptures, which are
able to make thee wise unto salvation
through faith which is in Christ Jesus."
2 Timothy 3:15

When the Philippian prison guard asked Paul,
"What must I do to be saved?," did Paul answer,
"You must become a member of the Roman
Catholic church?" No, he responded:

"***Believe*** on the Lord Jesus Christ, and
thou shalt be saved…"   Acts 16:31

Remember when Jesus was hanging on the cross?
The thief on the cross next to Him cried out:

"…Lord, remember me when thou
comest into thy kingdom." Luke 23:42

When that dying sinner uttered those words of
faith, Jesus responded by saying:

"To day shalt thou be with me in
paradise."   Luke 23:43

Salvation is in Christ… not in a church.

The catechism claims salvation comes "…through
Christ's Catholic Church alone…" But God's Word
says it is obtained through Jesus Christ:

"For the wages of sin is death; but the

gift of God is eternal life ***through
Jesus Christ our Lord.*** "Romans 6:23

"… God sent his only begotten Son
into the world, that we might live
through him."   1 John 4:9

Only Christ can offer us salvation because He
alone shed His blood for us:

"Much more then, being now justified by his blood, we shall be saved from
wrath ***through him.***"   Romans 5:9

No church can offer salvation. Only Jesus can:

"Neither is there salvation in ***any
other*** (except Jesus): for there is ***none***
other name under heaven given
among men, whereby we must be
saved."   Acts 4:10, 12

Conclusion

Since the Bible and Catholicism clearly disagree,
here are some questions you must answer:

• If the Catholic church is necessary to escape hell
and reach heaven, would not God have clearly
stated it in His Word… at least once?

• Why would Jesus repeatedly lie by saying that
salvation is available through faith in Him?

• Are you willing to call Jesus Christ, the Holy Spirit, the Apostle Paul and the Apostle John all liars? For your religion to be right, you must.

• For centuries, Bible believing Christians have contended that this unbiblical doctrine was created to keep members in bondage. Was it?

• Lastly, you must again answer the question, "Which will I obey and serve, the traditions of men, or the Word of God?" You cannot say "both" because each says the other is wrong.

Someday you will stand face to face with Jesus Christ. You will look Him right in the eyes. You might want to start thinking about how you are going to tell the Lord that you rejected His teachings and obeyed the traditions of sinful men because you assumed He was lying.

> "For laying aside the commandment
> of God, ye hold the tradition of
> men..."   Mark 7:8

2

Salvation Through Good Works

To be saved, Catholic doctrine requires the continual performance of good works.

> "Even though incorporated into the Church, one who does not however persevere in charity is not saved." Pg. 222, #837

These works include baptism (pg. 320, #1257), various sacraments (pg. 292, #1129) plus many additional works.

Once again the teachings of Catholicism oppose God's Word, which states that salvation **cannot** be earned, but is a free and undeserved gift of God:

> "For by grace are ye saved through faith; and that not of yourselves: it is the gift of God: **Not of works,** lest any man should boast."
>
> Ephesians 2:8-9

> ***"Not by works of righteousness***
> which we have done, but according to
> his mercy he saved us, by the washing
> of regeneration, and renewing of the
> Holy Ghost;"   Titus 3:5

The Bible repeatedly states that salvation comes through faith—never by good works:

> "Therefore we conclude that a man is
> justified by faith ***without the deeds of
> the law.***"   Romans 3:28

> "And the scripture, foreseeing that
> God would justify the heathen
> ***through faith...***"   Galatians 3:8

How do we become God's children?:

> "For ye are all the children of God ***by
> faith in Christ Jesus.***" Galatians 3:26

The Pharisees and good works

The religious Pharisees were convinced that performing good works would earn them salvation, but Jesus set them straight. In Mark's gospel, the Pharisees and scribes asked Jesus:

> "Why walk not thy disciples according
> to the tradition of the elders, but eat
> bread with unwashen hands?"
>
>   Mark 7:5

In response, Jesus chastised them:

> "Full well ye reject the commandment of God, that ye may keep your own tradition." Mark 7:9

What a tragedy! By elevating tradition above God's Word, the Pharisees had actually rejected the commandment of God. Jesus also accused the Pharisees of:

> "Making the word of God of none effect through your tradition…"
>
> Mark 7:13

This is exactly what the Catholic church does by elevating church tradition above the Word of God.

The Pharisees were convinced that salvation was obtained by performing good works, but good works can never save anybody:

> "Knowing that a man is **not** justified by the works of the law, but by the faith of Jesus Christ, even we have believed in Jesus Christ, that we might be justified by the faith of Christ, and not by the works of the law: for by the works of the law shall **no flesh be justified.**" Galatians 2:16

> "Therefore being justified ***by faith,***
> we have peace with God through our
> Lord Jesus Christ:"   Romans 5:1

Good works will not get you in

Many who stand before God will think they should enter heaven because of their good works. Jesus tells us in His Word:

> "Not every one that saith unto me,
> Lord, Lord, shall enter into the
> kingdom of heaven... ***Many*** will say
> to me in that day, Lord, Lord, have
> we not prophesied in thy name? and
> in thy name have cast out devils? and
> in thy name done many ***wonderful
> works***?"   Matthew 7:21-22

How shocked they will be when they hear Jesus respond:

> "I never knew you: depart from me,
> ye that work iniquity." Matthew 7:23

How tragic! Millions of Catholics never learn that good works cannot save them until after they die. But after death is too late. At that point they are already doomed to an eternity in the lake of fire.

The Apostle Paul makes another important statement concerning good works:

> "I do not frustrate the grace of God: for if righteousness come by the law, then Christ is dead in vain."
>
> Galatians 2:21

In other words, if you could earn heaven through your good works, then Jesus suffered that horrible death on the cross for nothing.

But He did not die in vain. Scripture declares that Jesus gave His life because there is **no other way** for our sins to be forgiven:

> "He that **believeth on him is not condemned:** but he that believeth not is condemned already, because he hath not believed in the name of the only begotten Son of God." John 3:18

Jesus repeats this same truth:

> "And this is the will of him that sent me, that every one which seeth the Son, and **believeth on him,** may have everlasting life..."   John 6:40

Conclusion

Roman Catholic friend, you must make another decision. Either you will believe God's Word and accept the **free** gift of salvation through faith alone in Jesus Christ, or you will believe the traditions of the Catholic church, that salvation must be earned through continual good works.

You cannot choose Catholic doctrine and God's Word because both disagree with each other.

My prayer is that you will make the right choice. If you choose to receive the God's free gift of salvation, before the end of the book, we will explain how you can do it:

> "Jesus answered and said unto them, This is the work of God, that ye ***believe on him*** whom he hath sent."
>
> John 6:29

3

The Church Forgives Sins

Catholicism teaches that *it* has the power and authority to forgive people's sins. Here are a few quotes from the Catechism. (Please note that whenever the Catechism mentions the "Church," it is referring to the "Roman Catholic church"):

> "There is no offense, however serious, that the Church cannot forgive." Pg. 256, #982

> "By Christ's will, the Church possesses the power to forgive the sins of the baptized..." Pg. 257, #986

> "The Church, who through the bishop and his priests forgives sins in the name of Jesus Christ..." Pg. 363-364, #1448

Does the Catholic church have power to forgive sins? Let's see what the Scriptures say:

> "Why doth this man thus speak blasphemies? who can forgive sins but ***God only?***"   Mark 2:7

> "And be ye kind one to another,
> tenderhearted, forgiving one another,
> even as *God for Christ's sake hath
> forgiven you.*"   Ephesians 4:32

According to Scripture, God wants His children to come straight to Him for forgiveness of sins, not to a church:

> *"Let us therefore come boldly unto
> the throne of grace,* that we may
> obtain mercy, and find grace to help
> in time of need."   Hebrews 4:16

This verse loudly proclaims that forgiveness of sins comes from God's throne, not from a church. Still, Catholicism teaches a contrary doctrine:

> "Indeed bishops and priests, by virtue of the sacrament of Holy Orders, have the power to forgive all sins 'in the name of the Father, and of the Son, and of the Holy Spirit.'" Pg. 367, #1461

> "The Church must be able to forgive all penitents their offenses, even if they should sin until the last moment of their lives." Pg. 255, #979

However, this man-made doctrine contradicts God's written Word. Many Bible characters freely approached God's throne for forgiveness of sins.

The psalmist went straight to God:

> "I acknowledged my sin unto thee... I
> said, I will confess my transgressions
> *unto the LORD;* and thou forgavest
> the iniquity of my sin..." Psalm 32:5

King David went directly to God to ask forgiveness for his sins:

> "Look upon mine affliction and my
> pain; and *forgive all my sins.*"
>   Psalm 25:18

In Psalm 51, David asks God for forgiveness again:

> "Wash me thoroughly from mine
> iniquity, and cleanse me from my sin.
> Against thee, thee only, have I sinned,
> and done this evil in thy sight..."
>   Psalm 51:2,4

King Solomon was also aware that he and all the children of Israel could go straight to God to get their sins forgiven:

> "Hearken therefore unto the suppli-
> cations of thy servant, and of thy
> people Israel, which they shall make
> toward this place: hear thou from thy
> dwelling place, even from heaven; and

when thou hearest, forgive."

2 Chronicles 6:21

God tells people to come to Him for forgiveness:

"If my people, which are called by my name, shall humble themselves, and pray, *and seek my face,* and turn from their wicked ways; *then will I hear from heaven, and will forgive their sin,* and will heal their land."

2 Chronicles 7:14

God never requires anyone to go through a church to obtain forgiveness for their sins.

"For thou, Lord, art good, and ready to forgive; and plenteous in mercy unto all them *that call upon thee.*"

Psalm 86:5

"... if any man have a quarrel against any: even *as Christ forgave you,* so also do ye."   Colossians 3:13

Why then would the Catholic church insist that forgiveness of sins is only available through her? The following Catechism quote provides the answer:

"Were there no forgiveness of sins in the Church, there would be no hope of life to come or eternal liberation. Let us thank God who has given his Church such a gift." Pg. 256, #983

Rather than looking to Jesus for forgiveness of sins and eternal life, Roman Catholics are taught that their sins can only be forgiven through the Catholic church. Whether intentional or not, this doctrine keeps people in bondage to the Catholic church.

Conclusion

Once again, God's Word stands on one side, while the traditions of men stand on the other. God says He alone forgives sins, while Catholic tradition contends that the Catholic church has the power to forgive sins. Which side will you choose?

> "Bless the LORD, O my soul, and forget not all his benefits: *Who forgiveth all thine iniquities...*"
>
> Psalm 103:2-3

4

The One True Church

Does Catholicism still teach that it is the one true Church founded by Christ? Many think not, but there is no denying the church's official position:

> "This is the sole Church of Christ, which in the Creed we profess to be one, holy, catholic and apostolic." Pg. 214, #811

Referring to the Catholic church, the Catechism pronounces:

> "In fact, in this one and only Church of God..." Pg. 216, #817

> "First, the Church is catholic because Christ is present in her. Where there is Christ Jesus, there is the Catholic Church." Pg. 220, #830

This "one true church" doctrine can be traced to one verse of Scripture, which, when compared with other Scriptures, is found not to teach this doctrine at all. When Jesus asked his disciples who He was, Peter responded:

> "Thou art the Christ, the Son of the
> living God.   Matthew 16:16

Then Jesus answered Peter:

> "… thou art Peter, and upon this rock
> I will build my church; and the gates
> of hell shall not prevail against it."
>   Matthew 16:18

Catholicism contends that the Lord was referring
to Peter as the rock, and has since built the entire
Catholic religion upon that premise. But all other
pertinent Scriptures declare that Jesus was referring to Himself as the rock, not Peter:

> "… for they drank of that spiritual
> Rock that followed them: and *that
> Rock was Christ.*" 1 Corinthians 10:4

Jesus is not only the rock, He is the chief cornerstone of the church:

> "And are built upon the foundation of
> the apostles and prophets, Jesus
> Christ himself being *the chief corner
> stone;*"   Ephesians 2:20

Back in the Old Testament, it was prophesied
that Jesus, whom men rejected, would become
the cornerstone of the church:

> "The stone which the builders refused

> is become the ***head stone of the corner.***"   Psalm 118:22

Even Peter, allegedly the first pope, confesses that Jesus Christ is the cornerstone of the church:

> "...by the name of Jesus Christ of Nazareth... This is the stone which was set at nought of you builders, which is become ***the head of the corner.***"   Acts 4:10-11

> "... the stone which the builders disallowed, the same is made ***the head of the corner,***"   1 Peter 2:7

According to Scriptures, Peter is NOT the rock:

> "For who is God save the LORD? or ***who is a rock save our God?***"
>
>   Psalm 18:31

> "... I will publish the name of the LORD: ascribe ye greatness unto our God. ***He is the Rock...***"
>
>   Deuteronomy 32:3-4

> "Truly my soul waiteth upon God... ***He only is my rock...***" Psalm 62:1-2

> "But the LORD is my defence; and ***my God is the rock of my refuge.***"
>
>   Psalm 94:22

Who is the head of the church

Despite all these Scriptures, Catholicism still claims that Peter was the rock and his successors are the head of the church:

"The sole Church of Christ (is that) which our Savior, after his Resurrection, entrusted to Peter's pastoral care, commissioning him and the other apostles to extend and rule it… This Church, constituted and organized as a society in the present world, subsists in (*subsistit in*) the Catholic Church, which is governed by the successors of Peter and by the bishops in communion with him." Pg. 215, #816

But the Bible declares that Jesus Christ, not Peter or his successors, is the head of the church:

"And *he (Christ) is the head of the body, the church:* who is the beginning, the firstborn from the dead; that in all things he (Christ) might have the preeminence."   Colossians 1:18

"And hath put all things under his feet, and gave him *(Christ) to be the head over all things* to the church,"
Ephesians 1:22

"But speaking the truth in love, may grow up into him in all things, which is ***the head, even Christ:"***

Ephesians 4:15

The biblical "church"

When the Bible uses the words "the church," it always refers to all those who trust in Jesus Christ alone for salvation, not just to members of the Catholic church:

> "Unto the church of God which is at Corinth, to them that are sanctified in Christ Jesus, called to be saints, with ***all that in every place call upon the name of Jesus Christ our Lord...***"

1 Corinthians 1:2

The Apostle Paul wrote:

> "Husbands, love your wives, even as Christ also ***loved the church,*** and gave himself for it;" Ephesians 5:25

Paul was not a Catholic, yet he knew that Christ loved him and died for him. Certainly, no one would dare say that Paul was not a Christian because he was not a Catholic.

Would anyone suggest that God only loves Catholics?... or that He only died for Catholics? Such would be the case if the Catholic church was the only church.

Paul also proclaimed:

> "And walk in love, as Christ also hath loved *us,* and hath given himself for *us...*"   Ephesians 5:2

Can non-Catholics be Christians?

As the "one true church," Catholicism claims the right to determine who is or is not a Christian:

> "All who have been justified by faith in Baptism are incorporated into Christ; they therefore have a right to be called Christians, and with good reason are accepted as brothers in the Lord by the children of the Catholic Church."
> Pg 216, #818

In other words, if you have not been baptized into the Catholic church, you are not a Christian. These are not my words, but the words of the official Catholic Catechism.

But according to Scripture, it doesn't matter if the Catholic church has accepted you or not. If your faith is in Jesus Christ alone, then He has already accepted you:

> "To the praise of the glory of his grace, wherein he *(Jesus) hath made us accepted* in the beloved."
>   Ephesians 1:6

Conclusion

At this point, you must make a few decisions:

• Is Peter really the rock? The Catechism says he is, but God's Word says he is not.

• Is the Catholic church the one true church? The Catechism says yes, but the Bible says no.

• Do you really believe that all non-Catholics will burn in hell?

Once again, the answers to each of these questions will be determined by which you choose to believe... the traditions of men, or God's Word. Jesus asked the Pharisees a question which all Roman Catholics should ponder:

> "Why do ye also transgress the commandment of God by your tradition?"
>   Matthew 15:3

5

Baptism Saves

The Catholic church contends that baptism is necessary for salvation:

> "The Lord himself affirms that Baptism is necessary for salvation." Pg. 320, #1257

All Catholics should be aware that the Lord does **not** agree with this statement. The Bible teaches that salvation is a free gift that works can never buy. This doctrine was devised by Catholicism:

> "The Church does not know of any other means other than Baptism that assures entry into eternal beatitude..." Pg. 320, #1257

> "The faithful are born anew by Baptism..." Pg. 311, #1212

> "Through Baptism we are freed from sin and reborn as sons of God; we become members of Christ, and are incorporated into the Church..." Pg. 312, #1213

The Bible could not disagree more:

> "But as many as ***received him,*** to them gave he power to become the sons of God, even to them that ***believe on his name:***"   John 1:12

Despite Bible verses like these, the Catechism teaches that:

> "Baptism not only purifies from all sins, but also makes the neophyte 'a new creature,' an adopted son of God, who has become a 'partaker of the divine nature,' member of Christ and co-heir with him, and a temple of the Holy Spirit." Pg. 322, #1265

> "By Baptism all sins are forgiven, original sin and all personal sins, as well as all punishment for sin." Pg. 321, #1263   (See pg. 257, #985)

All these doctrines violate a host of Scriptures. The Bible teaches that ***only Christ*** can forgive our sins, performing a "good work" like baptism will never do it:

> "In whom we have redemption through his (Christ's) blood, the forgiveness of sins…"   Ephesians 1:7

If baptism is necessary for salvation, would the Apostle Paul have proclaimed:

"For Christ sent me not to baptize,
but to preach the gospel…"
>   1 Corinthians 1:17

Or would this same great man of God have stated:

"I thank God that I baptized *none of
you,* but Crispus and Gaius;"
>   1 Corinthians 1:14

John the Baptist's message was:

"Repent ye: for the kingdom of heaven
is at hand."   Matthew 3:2

After people repented, then they were…

"… baptized of him in Jordan, con-
fessing their sins."   Matthew 3:6

Listen to what the Ethiopian eunuch asked Philip
as they discussed the subject of baptism:

"And as they went on their way, they
came unto a certain water: and the
eunuch said, See, here is water; what
doth hinder me to be baptized? And
Philip said, *If thou believest with all
thine heart,* thou mayest. And he
answered and said, I believe that Jesus
Christ is the Son of God."
>   Acts 8:36-37

The Bible teaches that baptism should occur after salvation, not as a requirement for salvation. When the Philippian jailer asked, "Sirs, what must I do to be saved?", Paul answered:

> "***Believe*** on the Lord Jesus Christ, and ***thou shalt be saved,*** and thy house... And he took them the same hour of the night, and washed their stripes; and was baptized, he and all his, straightway."   Acts 16:30, 31, 33

First, they believed, then they were baptized. Baptism always follows salvation! Here's another example:

> "And Crispus, the chief ruler of the synagogue, ***believed on the Lord*** with all his house; and many of the Corinthians hearing ***believed,*** and were baptized."   Acts 18:8

In Acts chapter two, Peter, the supposed first pope, preached. When he finished:

> "... they that gladly ***received his word*** were baptized: and the same day there were added unto them about three thousand souls."   Acts 2:41

Again, they were baptized, not to become sons of God, but because they already were sons of God.

When Philip preached to the people of Samaria, first came salvation, then baptism:

> "But when they **believed** Philip preaching the things concerning the kingdom of God, and the name of Jesus Christ, they were baptized, both men and women."   Acts 8:12

Soon after in that same passage, Simon, a deceiving sorcerer, followed the same path:

> "Then Simon himself **believed** also: and when he was baptized, he continued with Philip..."   Acts 8:13

The Catechism states:

> "All the sacraments are sacred links uniting the faithful with one another and binding them to Jesus Christ, and above all Baptism, the gate by which we enter into the Church." Pg. 248, #950

Just before his death, the thief on the cross next to Jesus put his faith in Jesus Christ. Obviously, he was never baptized, but he still went to paradise. Why? Because salvation is through faith in Christ, not through baptism.

The Catechism also contends that when a person is baptized, it is really Jesus Himself who is doing the baptizing:

"By his (Christ's) power he is present in the sacraments so that when anybody baptizes, it is really Christ himself who baptizes." Pg. 283, #1088

Simply stated, this is another Catholic tradition not found in God's Word.

Another Contradiction

Here is another Catholic doctrine:

"Baptism indeed is the seal of eternal life." Pg. 324, #1274

But the Bible disagrees again, stating that the eternal destiny of God's children has been sealed with the Holy Spirit:

"… in whom also after that ye believed, *ye were sealed with that holy Spirit* of promise,"   Ephesians 1:13

"And grieve not the holy Spirit of God, whereby ye are *sealed* unto the day of redemption."   Ephesians 4:30

Conclusion

Is baptism necessary for salvation? Catholic tradition and God's Word are at odds. The Catechism says "yes." God's Word says "no."

Who will you believe?

6

The Pope:
Vicar of Christ

Is the pope the vicar (substitute) of Christ on the earth, wielding universal power over the whole church? If you believe the catechism, he is:

> "For the Roman Pontiff, by reason of his office as Vicar of Christ, and as pastor of the entire Church has full, supreme, and universal power over the whole Church, a power which he can always exercise unhindered." Pg. 234, #882

> "The Roman Pontiff... as supreme pastor and teacher of all the faithful..." Pg. 235, #891

While the Catholic church elevates the pope to the position of "supreme pastor and teacher of all the faithful," God's Word reveals that someone else already fills that position:

> "But the Comforter, which is the Holy Ghost, whom the Father will

> send in my name, *he shall teach you
> all things,* and bring all things to
> your remembrance, whatsoever I have
> said unto you."   John 14:26

> "Howbeit when he, the Spirit of
> truth, is come, *he will guide you into
> all truth...*"   John 16:13

Jesus promised that this infallible teacher would
abide with us forever:

> "And I will pray the Father, and he
> shall give you another Comforter, that
> he may abide with you *for ever;"*
>
>   John 14:16

The pope has clearly assumed a position reserved
for the Holy Spirit of God. It is a position no
man can fill:

> "For what man knoweth the things of
> a man, save the spirit of man which is
> in him? even so the things of God
> knoweth *no man,* but the Spirit of
> God."   1 Corinthians 2:11

The Apostle Paul reiterates that the Holy Spirit of
God, not a man, is the infallible teacher of all
true Christians:

> "Now we have received, not the spirit

of the world, but *the spirit which is of God;* that we might know the things that are freely given to us of God. Which things also we speak, not in the words which man's wisdom teacheth, but which *the Holy Ghost teacheth*..."   1 Corinthians 2:12-13

Similarities?

If the pope is Christ's substitute on earth, there should be many similarities in their lives. Let's see:

• While on earth, Jesus never controlled great wealth. The pope controls one of the wealthiest corporations in the world.

• Jesus dressed like a common man. The pope, on the other hand, is never seen in anything but regal apparel.

• Jesus lived in simple surroundings, but the pope views opulence at every turn.

• Jesus tirelessly served the multitudes, while the pope travels the world on his private jet, meeting with world leaders from every nation.

• Most people eventually rejected and hated Jesus because He told the truth. The pope is worshipped and adored by millions worldwide.

• The pope gladly welcomes the praise of men, but Jesus directed all worship to the Father, and said of Himself:

> "Why callest thou me good? there is none good but one, that is, God."
>
> Mark 10:18

Should popes accept the worship of multitudes? Look how "Pope" Peter reacted when Cornelius tried to worship him:

> "And as Peter was coming in, Cornelius met him, and fell down at his feet, and worshipped him. But Peter took him up, saying, Stand up; I myself also am a man." Acts 10:25-26

Pope: head of the church?

The Catechism claims that:

> "The Pope enjoys, by divine institution, supreme, full, immediate, and universal power in the care of souls" Pg. 246, #937

According to God's Word, the pope is **not** the head of the true church of Jesus Christ. That position is reserved exclusively for the Lord Jesus:

> "For the husband is the head of the wife, even as *Christ is the head of the church*..." Ephesians 5:23

Concerning the pope's title of "Holy Father," Jesus Himself instructed us to:

> "…call no man your father upon the earth: for one is your Father, which is in heaven."   Matthew 23:9

Yet, the pope not only accepts the title "Father," but "Holy Father" as well, a title reserved for God alone:

> "Who shall not fear thee, O Lord, and glorify thy name? for *thou only art holy…*"   Revelation 15:4

It is not wise to assume a name reserved for God, for He will not share His glory with anyone:

> "I am the LORD: that is my name: and *my glory will I not give to another…*"   Isaiah 42:8

More Nagging Questions

Once again, Catholic doctrine and Scriptures could not disagree more. As a result, you must choose sides on each of the following questions:

• Why didn't God tell us in the Bible that He was sending the pope as the Vicar of Christ?

• Why does the Bible insist that Jesus is still the head of the church, if He isn't?

• Why does the Catholic church want the pope to be the final authority instead of Jesus?

• Why does the Catholic church want the pope to be your teacher instead of the Holy Spirit of God?

Conclusion

Only you can answer these questions for yourself. And only you can decide which side you will believe—Catholic traditions of men... or God's Word?

> "And ye are complete in him (Jesus), which is *the head of all principality and power:*"   Colossians 2:10

> "And he (Christ) is *the head* of the body, the church..."   Colossians 1:18

7

The Pope: Infallible

According to Catholic doctrine, the Pope is infallible in matters of doctrine, faith and morals.

"In order to preserve the Church in the purity of the faith handed on by the apostles, Christ who is Truth willed to confer on her a share in his own infallibility. By a supernatural sense of faith the People of God, under the guidance of the Church's living magisterium, unfailingly adheres to this faith." Pg. 235, #889

The Catechism restates the same belief this way:

"The Roman Pontiff... enjoys this infallibility in virtue of his office, when, as supreme pastor and teacher of all the faithful – who confirms his brethren in the faith – he proclaims by a definitive act a doctrine pertaining to faith or morals... This infallibility extends as far as the deposit of divine Revelation itself." Pg. 235, #891

Sadly, this doctrine is but another tradition of men that contradicts Scripture. The Bible declares that *all* people are sinners. No one is perfect or infallible in anything:

> "For *all* have sinned, and come short of the glory of God;"   Romans 3:23

> "As it is written, There is *none* righteous, *no, not one:*"   Romans 3:10

Notice, you didn't read, "no one, except the pope." Jesus is the only infallible person who ever lived:

> "For he (God) hath made him (Jesus) to be sin for us, *who knew no sin...*"
> 2 Corinthians 5:21

Are other Catholics infallible too?

The Catechism further alleges that other Catholic leaders have also somehow achieved this state of infallibility:

> "The pastoral duty of the Magisterium is aimed at seeing to it that the People of God abides in the truth that liberates. To fulfill this service, Christ endowed the Church's shepherds with the charism of infallibility in matters of faith and morals." Pg. 235, #890

> "The infallibility of the Magisterium of the

> Pastors extends to all the elements of doctrine, including moral doctrine, without which the saving truths of the faith cannot be preserved, expounded, or observed." Pg. 495, #2051

It is important to understand that God did not declare these people to be infallible, other sinful men did.

Scriptures overflow with stories of sinful people. Even those whom God used the most were sinners. God referred to King David as "a man after mine own heart" (Acts 13:22), yet David was a murderer and an adulterer, among other things.

The Apostle Paul and all the other apostles were sinners. Paul said of himself:

> "Unto me, who am *less than the least of all saints,* is this grace given, that I should preach among the Gentiles the unsearchable riches of Christ;"
>
> Ephesians 3:8

Nobody in Scripture, except Jesus, was infallible.

More questions

Aside from being unscriptural, this far reaching doctrine raises other important questions which you must answer for yourself:

• When the pope and other Catholic leaders, who

claim to be infallible, disagree with God's Holy Word, then God must be wrong. Are you willing to accept this?

• Why does the Catholic church want you to believe that the pope and other Catholic leaders are infallible in matters of doctrine? Is it to bring members into further bondage and obedience to the Catholic church?

• Where do fallible men obtain the authority to declare other men infallible?

• Why does the Catholic church refuse to honor Jesus Christ by acknowledging Him as the only infallible One, as the Holy Scriptures teach?

Conclusion

Here is another tradition of men that raises more questions than it answers.

Please don't blindly accept this Catholic doctrine as truth. Look to God's Word for answers to these questions, then settle this issue in your own heart:

> "And being made *perfect,* he (Jesus) became the author of eternal salvation unto all them that obey him;"
>
> Hebrews 5:9

8

The Sacraments Save

Are the sacraments necessary for salvation?

"The Church affirms that for believers the sacraments of the New Covenant are necessary for salvation." Pg. 292, #1129

What are the sacraments?:

"There are seven sacraments in the Church: Baptism, Confirmation or Chrismation, Eucharist, Penance, Anointing of the Sick, Holy Orders, and Matrimony." Pg. 289, #1113

These seven sacraments are nothing more than a series of good works. As we have already seen in previous chapters, the Bible states repeatedly that good works will never save anybody:

"Therefore by the deeds of the law there shall **no flesh be justified** in his sight…"   Romans 3:20

Here is what God thinks of our good works:

> "But we are all as an unclean thing, and all our righteousnesses are as *filthy rags...*" Isaiah 64:6

Must one be a Catholic to be saved?

Since the sacraments are supposedly necessary for salvation, and since the sacraments are only available through the Catholic church, then obviously, one must be a faithful member of the Catholic church to be saved.

Though you will never hear a spokesperson for Catholicism admit it, this is exactly what this Catholic doctrine purports.

I ask you again, can you accept that everyone outside the Catholic church will burn forever in hell?

Traditions of men

Please understand, these sacraments, which the Catholic church contends are necessary for salvation, did not even come from God. They are man-made rules which have been handed down through generations.

So when you perform them, you are not obeying God, you are obeying the traditions of men.

One must wonder, under such conditions, if these sacraments are really necessary, or if the Catholic church is using man's traditions to scare people into lifelong obedience to the church, under the threat of eternal damnation.

Salvation: through Christ or sacraments?

If sacraments are necessary for salvation, why does God's Word proclaim the following?

> "But these are written, that ye might believe that Jesus is the Christ, the Son of God; and that ***believing*** ye might have life ***through his name.***"
>
> John 20:31

Paul, the Apostle, delivered these sobering words on the subject:

> "For the preaching of the cross is to them that perish foolishness; but unto us which are saved it is the power of God."   1 Corinthians 1:18

Catholic friend: do you believe that good works like the sacraments are necessary for salvation? Do you consider it foolishness to believe that salvation can only be obtained through faith in Christ's work on the cross? If so, God's Word warns that you will perish in hell.

When Jesus declared that salvation came only through Him, not only was He telling the truth, He was repeating what He heard from the Father:

> "But now ye seek to kill me, a man that hath **told you the truth, which I have heard of God..."** John 8:40

To suggest that Jesus is wrong is to suggest that the Father is wrong, as well. Jesus goes on to explain why people refuse to believe His Words:

> "He that is of God heareth God's words: ye therefore hear them not, **because ye are not of God."** John 8:47

To accept this Catholic doctrine, you must refuse to hear God's Words. Jesus said that if you can do this, then you are not of God.

Are you sure, beyond any shadow of a doubt, Roman Catholic friend, that you are of God?

Are you willing to turn your back on God's Word to accept man's words. If you can, you have reason for grave concern:

> "Then Peter and the other apostles answered and said, **We ought to obey God rather than men."** Acts 5:29

9

The Sin of Presumption

Catholicism maintains that believing you are assured of going to heaven when you die is to commit the sin of presumption:

> "There are two kinds of presumption. Either man presumes upon his own capacities, (hoping to be able to save himself without help from on high), or he presumes upon God's almighty power or his mercy (hoping to obtain his forgiveness without conversion and glory without merit." Pg. 507, #2092

By taking this position, the Catholic church once again lines itself up against written Scripture:

> "These things have I written unto you that believe on the name of the Son of God; that ye may **know that ye have eternal life,** and that ye may believe on the name of the Son of God."
>
> 1 John 5:13

Stop and reason for a moment. If there is a place called heaven, a paradise wonderful beyond imagination, and if there is a place of eternal torment called hell, wouldn't a loving God tell us how to obtain one and avoid the other?

Would God make us endure an entire lifetime, never knowing how we could escape the flames of hell and be assured of enjoying paradise with Him?

Would a loving God say, "Do as many good works as you can, then keep your fingers crossed and hope for the best when you stand before Me someday."

No, that's not love, that's torture! That's cruelty of the highest sort. A God of love would give us a clear, simple plan spelling out how to miss this awful place of torment and be assured of heaven. And He has:

> "For God so loved the world, that he gave his only begotten Son, that whosoever **believeth in him** should not perish, but **have everlasting life.**"
>
> John 3:16

The Bible declares that those who receive Christ by faith and put their trust in Him can know right now that they have eternal life:

> "He that believeth on the Son ***hath
> everlasting life:*** and he that believeth
> not the Son shall not see life; but the
> wrath of God abideth on him."
>
> John 3:36

> "He that heareth my word, and be-
> lieveth on him that sent me, ***hath
> everlasting life,*** and shall not come
> into condemnation; but is passed
> from death unto life."   John 5:24

It's not a sin to presume you are going to heaven
if you have been born into God's family through
faith in Christ. It is a Biblical fact and a precious
promise from the Lord Jesus. It is never presumptuous to take God at His Word. In fact, He
loves it when we do:

> "My sheep hear my voice, and I know
> them, and they follow me: And I give
> unto them eternal life; and ***they shall
> never perish,*** neither shall any man
> pluck them out of my hand."
>
> John 10:27-28

God wants His children to rest in the fact that
they have been born into His family and that
their eternal destiny is settled:

> "Verily, verily, I say unto you, He that believeth on me *hath everlasting life."*   John 6:47

Notice, the promise is not that you may have it someday if you do enough good works. You may have it *right now.* This is God's will. Jesus said:

> "And this is the will of him that sent me, that every one which seeth the Son, and *believeth on him,* may have everlasting life: and I will raise him up at the last day."   John 6:40

Paul didn't consider it presumptuous to declare that he was on his way to heaven:

> "For I am in a strait betwixt two, having a desire to depart, and to be with Christ; which is far better:"
>
>   Philippians 1:23

Precious Roman Catholic, can't you see that this doctrine keeps you in bondage? The church doesn't want you to know your eternal destiny is settled because you'd no longer need the church.

How tragic that Catholics remain in bondage, serving the church in hopes of earning heaven, when God's desire is for you to be assured of heaven right now:

"In hope of eternal life, which God, that cannot lie, ***promised*** before the world began;" Titus 1:2

"And this is the promise that he hath promised us, ***even eternal life.***"
1 John 2:25

You must be born again

To have this assurance, you must be born again:

"Jesus answered and said unto him, Verily, verily, I say unto thee, Except a man be born again, he cannot see the kingdom of God." John 3:3

To be born again, you must receive Jesus Christ by faith as your personal Savior and trust Him alone for your salvation. When you do this, you will be born into God's family:

"But as many as received him, to them gave he power to become the sons of God, even to them that believe on his name:" John 1:12

Once in God's family, you become a co-heir with Jesus Christ:

"And if children, then heirs; heirs of God, and joint-heirs with Christ…"
Romans 8:17

As an heir, you don't have to wonder about your destiny. You are promised:

> "...an inheritance incorruptible, and undefiled, and that fadeth not away, ***reserved in heaven for you,***"
>
> 1 Peter 1:4

Isn't that beautiful? An eternal inheritance in heaven is already reserved for all those who become a child of God. Jesus reminded those who trusted in Him that:

> "In my Father's house are many mansions: if it were not so, I would have told you. I go to prepare a place for you."
>
> John 14:2

Are you seeing the true nature of God? He loves you and wants you to know that it is not presumptuous to believe His Word and rest in His goodness. God loves you and wants you to ***know*** that you have eternal life... right now!

The bondage can be broken

God doesn't want you in bondage to a religion of works. He wants to have a personal relationship with you based on His wonderful grace. God doesn't want you to be tortured, wondering where you will spend eternity.

Ask God to open your eyes so you can see this awesome truth. Then receive Jesus by saying a prayer like this from your heart:

> Dear Heavenly Father:
>
> I admit that I have put my faith in a religion and not in you. I have been trying to earn heaven by obeying the good works of my church. But now I see that good works will never get me to heaven. Only by accepting Jesus will I gain eternal life.
>
> Right now, I ask Jesus Christ to come into my heart and save me. I repent of my sins and I repent of having put my faith in the Roman Catholic church. From now on I will trust in Jesus Christ alone.
>
> Thank you for showing me the truth and for saving my soul. Thank you for giving me the assurance of heaven. In Jesus' name, Amen.

If you just prayed a prayer like this and meant it with all your heart, God has promised that you are now His child and are guaranteed of going to heaven when you die.

Presumption or Faith?

It is not presumptuous to take God at His Word. That is called faith. When Jesus walked the earth, He gave all who put their faith in Him this wonderful promise:

> "And if I go and prepare a place for you, I will come again, and receive you unto myself; that where I am, there ye may be also." John 14:3

Trust Christ right now. You'll be glad you did:

> "For the LORD loveth judgment, and forsaketh not his saints; *they are preserved for ever:* but the seed of the wicked shall be cut off."
>
> Psalm 37:28

10

Infant Baptism

Infant Baptism is one of the most critical doctrines of the Catholic church:

> "Born with a fallen human nature and tainted by original sin, children also have need of the new birth in Baptism to be freed from the power of darkness and brought into the realm of the freedom of the children of God, to which all men are called. The sheer gratuitousness of the grace of salvation is particularly manifest in infant Baptism. The Church and the parents would deny a child the priceless grace of becoming a child of God were they not to confer Baptism shortly after birth." Pg. 319, #1250

The Catechism tells us where this cornerstone doctrine originated:

> "The practice of infant Baptism is an immemorial **tradition of the Church.** There is explicit testimony to this practice from the second century on..." Pg. 319, #1252
>
> *(Emphasis author's)*

Here, the Catechism admits that this doctrine is not based upon Scripture. It is a man-made tradition. Paul's warning might fit well here:

> "Beware lest any man spoil you through philosophy and vain deceit, after the tradition of men, after the rudiments of the world, and not after Christit."   Colossians 2:8

Baptism in the Bible

What makes this practice especially disturbing is that the Bible does not record a single occurance of an infant being baptized. On the contrary, every mention of baptism involves people old enough to hear and receive the gospel.

Jesus was an adult when he was baptized:

> "… Jesus, when he was baptized, went up straightway out of the water…"
>
> Matthew 3:16

Throughout the Bible, baptism always followed salvation. The Ethiopian eunuch who was led to salvation by Philip was an adult when he was baptized:

> "… they went down both into the water, both Philip and the eunuch; and he baptized him."   Acts 8:38

Others were baptized after they believed:

> "And Crispus, the chief ruler of the synagogue, ***believed on the Lord*** with all his house; and many of the Corinthians hearing ***believed,*** and were baptized." Acts 18:8

After people heeded John the Baptist's message to "repent," they were:

> "... baptized of him in Jordan, confessing their sins." Matthew 3:6

Obviously, newborn infants cannot repent, believe or confess their sins. Therefore, they are never qualified to be scripturally baptized.

The Philippian jailer

When the Philippian jailer who guarded the Apostle Paul asked, "What must I do to be saved?" (Acts 16:30), Paul answered, "Believe on the Lord Jesus Christ (v. 31)." After the jailer believed, Paul baptized him (v. 33).

When Peter preached in Acts, chapter two:

> "... they that gladly ***received his word*** were baptized: and the same day there were added unto them about three thousand souls." Acts 2:41

When Philip preached to the people of Samaria, men and women were baptized, but no infants were baptized:

> "But when they believed Philip preaching the things concerning the kingdom of God, and the name of Jesus Christ, they were baptized, ***both men and women.***"   Acts 8:12

If God's Word is so explicit that only those old enough to hear and receive God's Word should be baptized, then why does Catholicism demand that newborn infants be baptized? Is it to bring people into bondage to the church from shortly after their birth? You must settle this question in your own heart.

Conclusion

When you were baptized as an infant, were you really baptized, or did you merely have some water sprinkled on you? It all depends on which side you will believe in—the Word of God or the traditions of men. Please keep in mind the words Jesus spoke to the religious leaders of His day:

> "Full well ye reject the commandment of God, that ye may keep your own tradition."   Mark 7:9

11

Degrees of Sin

The Catechism indoctrinates Catholics with the notion that there are varying degrees of sin:

> "Sins are rightly evaluated according to their gravity." Pg. 454, #1854

First are venial sins:

> "One commits venial sin when, in a less serious matter, he does not observe the standard prescribed by the moral law, or when he disobeys the moral law in a grave manner, but without full knowledge or without complete consent." Pg. 456, #1862

Then there are mortal sins:

> "Mortal sin... results in the loss of charity and the privation of sanctifying grace, that is, of the state of grace. If it is not redeemed by repentance and God's forgiveness, it causes exclusion from Christ's kingdom and the eternal death of hell..." Pg. 456, #1861

(See also Pg. 264, #1014, Pg. 269, #1033, Pg. 270, #1035 and Pg. 270, #1037.)

With the threat of "the eternal death of hell" hanging over your head, several important questions need answers, like:

- What specifically constitutes a mortal sin?
- How much repentance does it take to get one forgiven?
- How do I know when one is forgiven?
- Why is the Bible silent on the subject?

Tragically, the Catechism does not provide answers to any of these questions.

What does the Bible teach?

When we turn to God's Holy Word, we get a totally different picture:

> "Whosoever committeth sin transgresseth also the law: for *sin is the transgression of the law.*" 1 John 3:4

Since we have all broken a command of God, the Bible declares that we are all sinners.

> "For *all have sinned,* and come short of the glory of God." Romans 3:23

Because of sin we all deserve to die and suffer the punishment of hell:

> *"The wages of sin is death…"*
>
> Romans 6:23

God's Word makes no distinction as to the gravity of certain sins. It simply states that the wages of *sin* is death.

But God in His great grace and love, sent His Son, Jesus Christ, to die on the cross to pay the price for *all* sin once and for all:

> "But this man (Jesus), after he had offered one sacrifice for sins for ever, sat down on the right hand of God;"
>
> Hebrews 10:12

True salvation is only available through Jesus Christ because only He could shed sinless blood to pay the penalty for all sin:

> "In whom we have redemption through his blood, even *the forgiveness of sins:"* Colossians 1:14

> "For this is my blood of the new testament, which is shed for many for *the remission of sins."*
>
> Matthew 26:28

While God does expect His children to confess their sins to Him, once sins are confessed and forgiven, God makes a wonderful promise:

"And their sins and iniquities will I remember no more."   Hebrews 10:17

Jesus is demoted again

Here again, honor is stolen from Jesus Christ. Because of the Lord's selfless act of love on the cross, He alone deserves credit for remitting the sins of all mankind.

Catholicism, though, demotes the Lord and robs Him of the honor and glory that He alone deserves, by declaring that lowly sinners can help pay for varying degrees of sins through their good works.

Conclusion

Again you must choose. Will you remain in bondage to Catholicism by believing that some sins are worse than others and that continual good works are needed to pay for these various degrees of sin?

Or will you trust God's Word, that Jesus died to pay the price for all sin, once and for all?

> "For I delivered unto you first of all that which I also received, how that ***Christ died for our sins*** according to the scriptures;"   1 Corinthians 15:3

12

Transubstantiation

During the mass, priests allegedly have the power to supernaturally turn the bread and wine into the actual and literal body and blood of Jesus Christ:

> "The Council of Trent summarizes the Catholic faith by declaring: "Because Christ our Redeemer said that it was truly his body that he was offering under the species of bread, it has always been the conviction of the Church of God, and this holy Council now declares again, that by the consecration of the bread and wine there takes place a change of the whole substance of the bread into the substance of the body of Christ our Lord and of the whole substance of the wine into the substance of his blood. This change the holy Catholic Church has fittingly and properly called transubstantiation." Pg. 347, #1376.

This Catechism quote reveals that the Catholic

church still adheres to this doctrine which was
defined at the Council of Trent:

> "At the heart of the Eucharistic celebration are
> the bread and wine that, by the words of Christ
> and the invocation of the Holy Spirit, become
> Christ's Body and Blood." Pg. 336 # 1333

The Catechism even specifies when Christ comes
into the eucharist and how long He stays:

> "The Eucharistic presence of Christ begins at
> the moment of the consecration and endures as
> long as the Eucharistic species subsist. Christ is
> present whole and entire in each of the species
> and whole and entire in each of their parts, in
> such a way that the breaking of the bread does
> not divide Christ." Pg. 347 #1377

Since Catholicism is teaching members to partake
in literal cannibalism, this doctrine requires
serious examination. To begin with, we must
determine this doctrine's origin. Is it from God,
or is it a tradition of men? Catholicism insists it is
scriptural, citing the words of Jesus in John 6:

> "Except ye eat the flesh of the Son of
> man, and drink his blood, ye have no
> life in you. Whoso eateth my flesh,
> and drinketh my blood, hath eternal
> life; and I will raise him up at the last
> day."   John 6:53-54

Though this one verse does appear to teach cannibalism, if you read the entire passage in context, the meaning becomes clear. Right before making that statement, Jesus said:

> "… For the bread of God is he which cometh down from heaven, and giveth life unto the world. Then said they unto him, Lord, evermore give us this bread. And Jesus said unto them, I am the bread of life: he that cometh to me shall never hunger; and he that **believeth on me** shall never thirst." John 6:33-35

This teaching is consistent with the rest of Scripture. Eternal life comes through believing in Jesus Christ, not eating His body. The Lord goes on to further clarify:

> "And this is the will of him that sent me, that every one which seeth the Son, and **believeth on him, may have everlasting life…**" John 6:40

Again, Jesus points out that eternal life comes through believing in Him. When the Lord's disciples murmured at His words, Jesus explained:

> "It is the spirit that quickeneth; the flesh profiteth nothing: the words that

> I speak unto you, ***they are spirit,*** and
> they are life."   John 6:63

Jesus was talking spiritually, not physically. He was explaining that spiritually, all life comes through faith in Him, not eating His body.

Nowhere else in the Bible does God endorse cannibalism. In fact, God forbids the practice:

> "But flesh with the life thereof, which
> is the blood thereof, ***shall ye not eat.***"
> Genesis 9:4

> "... ***No soul of you shall eat blood,***
> neither shall any stranger that sojourn-
> eth among you eat blood."
> Leviticus 17:12

God would never command His children to do something He had already forbidden.

The Biblical purpose

Paul's instructions in 1 Corinthians 11 shed even more light on this matter:

> "For I have received of the Lord that
> which also I delivered unto you, That
> the Lord Jesus the same night in
> which he was betrayed took bread:
> And when he had given thanks, he
> brake it, and said, Take, eat: this is my

body, which is broken for you: ***this do
in remembrance of me.***"

1 Corinthians 11:23-24

When Jesus said, "Take, eat: this is my body," He
was not suggesting that they reach out and begin
eating His literal body. To even suggest such is
ridiculous. He was speaking spiritually about
what He was about to accomplish on the cross.

Notice how that verse ends: "…this do in remembrance of me." Observing the Lord's Supper
is a ***remembrance*** of Christ's work at Calvary, not
a reenactment. The same is true of Christ's blood:

> "After the same manner also he took
> the cup, when he had supped, saying,
> This cup is the new testament in my
> blood: this do ye, as oft as ye drink it,
> ***in remembrance of me.***"

1 Corinthians 11:25

Jesus Himself taught the same lesson to his
disciples at the Last Supper:

> "And he (Jesus) took bread, and gave
> thanks, and brake it, and gave unto
> them, saying, This is my body which
> is given for you: ***this do in remem-
> brance of me.***"   Luke 22:19

Conclusion

Since transubstantiation is another unscriptural Catholic tradition of men, several more intriguing questions await an answer:

• Why does the Catholic church deliberately take one verse of Scripture out of context and build a doctrine the Bible obviously does not teach?

• Why would the Catholic church rather have you eating God than placing your faith in Him?

• Most importantly, can you knowingly partake in this practice now that you know the truth?

> "Therefore to him that knoweth to do good, and doeth it not, to him it is sin."　　　　　　James 4:17

13

Eucharist: Preserves from Sin

Does partaking of the Eucharist have power to cleanse Catholics from past sins and preserve them from future sins?

> "For this reason the Eucharist cannot unite us to Christ without at the same time cleansing us from past sins and preserving us from future sins:" Pg. 351, #1393

> "By the same charity that it enkindles in us, the Eucharist preserves us from future mortal sins." Pg. 352, #1395

Once again, God's Word and Catholic tradition couldn't be farther apart. Regarding cleansing from past sins, the Bible declares that all sins are washed away through the blood of Jesus Christ:

> "...*the blood* of Jesus Christ his Son *cleanseth us from all sin.*" 1 John 1:7

> "And from Jesus Christ, who is the

> faithful witness…Unto him that loved
> us, and ***washed us from our sins in
> his own blood,***"   Revelation 1:5

The Catechism strips away from Christ the credit
He alone deserves for cleansing people from their
sins, and credits instead a wafer with accomplish-
ing that task. Why is Jesus demoted again?

> "And such were some of you: but ye
> are ***washed,*** but ye are sanctified, but
> ye are justified ***in the name of the
> Lord Jesus,*** and by the Spirit of our
> God."   1 Corinthians 6:11

Preserving from future sins

There is no scriptural evidence that eating a piece
of bread will preserve anyone from future sins.
This doctrine's only practical function is to keep
members returning to the Catholic church to
receive the Eucharist, in hopes that it will help
preserve them from sin.

Aside from holding people in bondage to the
church, there is little else such a practice can
accomplish.

Though God's Word does not endorse this
practice, it does suggest a way you can protect
yourself from sin:

"Thy word have I hid in mine heart,
that I might not sin against thee."
Psalm 119:11

"Wherewithal shall a young man
cleanse his way? *by taking heed
thereto according to thy word."*
Psalm 119:9

To preserve yourself from sin, God suggests that
you read, memorize and obey the Bible. Curiously,
the Catholic church disagrees. It seems that the
Catholic leadership would rather have you
looking to the church for help than to God's
Word.

You must decide why:

"The LORD shall *preserve thee from
all evil…*"
Psalm 121:7

"Thou art my hiding place; thou shalt
preserve me from trouble; thou shalt
compass me about with songs of
deliverance. Selah."
Psalm 32:7

"And the Lord shall deliver me from
every evil work, and will *preserve me*
unto his heavenly kingdom: to whom
be glory for ever and ever. Amen."
2 Timothy 4:18

Conclusion

To cleanse you from past sins and protect you from future sins, Catholicism demands that you look to a piece of bread.

It is imperative that you understand that this tradition of men directly contradicts God's Word. To obey this Catholic doctrine, you must reject Holy Scriptures.

Do you really want to do this?

> "Now *unto him that is able to keep you from falling,* and to present you faultless before the presence of his glory with exceeding joy, To the only wise God our Saviour, be glory and majesty, dominion and power, both now and ever. Amen."   Jude 1:24-25

14

Eucharist: Helps the Dead

Partaking of the Eucharist purportedly gives Catholics who are still alive an opportunity to help the dead:

> "The Eucharistic sacrifice is also offered for the faithful departed who 'have died in Christ but are not yet wholly purified, so that they may be able to enter into the light and peace of Christ.'" Pg. 345, #1371

> "In the Eucharist, the Church expresses her efficacious communion with the departed..." Pg. 420 #1689

This heart-tugging doctrine indoctrinates Roman Catholics with the belief that regularly receiving the Eucharist will help their departed loved ones reach heaven faster.

If this doctrine is of God, then you should obey it. But if it's a tradition devised by men to keep people in bondage to a church, then it is a cruel and heartless method of controlling people. Let's see what God says about it.

Never mentioned

You can search the Scriptures from beginning to end, but you will not find the Eucharist helping a single dead person. And not one Bible character ever received the Eucharist on behalf of a departed loved one.

As you may suspect, this Catholic tradition is not only absent from God's Word, it directly violates it as well. The Bible teaches that we will each give account for our own life:

> "So then every one of us shall give account of *himself* to God."
> Romans 14:12

Jesus did all the work

People enter heaven solely because of the good work Jesus Christ did on the cross. Salvation is a gift from God, not an item earned by our righteousness or the righteousness of friends and loved ones.

Death, then judgment

The Bible declares that after death, everyone faces God for judgment. There are no more chances:

> "And as it is appointed unto men once
> to die, *but after this the judgment:*"
> Hebrews 9:27

Those who do not put their faith in Christ while they are alive are already condemned to hell:

> "He that believeth on him (Jesus) is
> not condemned: but he that believeth
> not *is condemned already,* because
> he hath not believed in the name of
> the only begotten Son of God."
> John 3:18

The wrath of God abides on those who die without Christ:

> "He that believeth on the Son hath
> everlasting life: and he that believeth
> not the Son shall not see life; but *the
> wrath of God abideth on him.*"
> John 3:36

The Bible says nothing about God's wrath being pacified because someone received the Eucharist on behalf of departed loved ones. The only way to avoid the condemnation of God is by placing your faith in Jesus Christ while you are alive. Jesus declared:

> "... He that heareth my word, and

believeth on him that sent me, hath everlasting life, and *shall not come into condemnation;* but is passed from death unto life."

John 5:24

Conclusion

Once again, you are left with several questions which must be answered:

• Why is this tradition of the Catholic church so diametrically opposed to God's Holy Word?

• Why does the Catholic church want members performing rituals for the dead, when God's Word says such practices are useless?

• Is this but another method of keeping people in bondage to the Catholic church?

Most importantly, you need to understand that to continue practicing this man-made tradition, you must reject the very words of Jesus Christ. Are you sure you want to do this?

"Beware lest any man spoil you through philosophy and vain deceit, after the tradition of men, after the rudiments of the world, and not after Christ."   Colossians 2:8

15

Mary Saves

Does Mary, the mother of Jesus, play a role in the salvation of mankind?:

> "Taken up to heaven she (Mary) did not lay aside this saving office but by her manifold intercession continues to bring us the gifts of eternal salvation…" Pg. 252, #969

> "Being obedient she (Mary) became the cause of salvation for herself and for the whole human race." Pg. 125, #494

Is this doctrine scriptural? According to God's Word, Mary has never had anything to do with the salvation process. Scripture reveals that Jesus is the ONLY One who can provide salvation:

> "Neither is there salvation in any other: for there is *none other name* under heaven given among men, whereby we must be saved." Acts 4:12

Jesus Himself declared that He is the ONLY way to heaven:

> "Jesus saith unto him, I am the way, the truth, and the life: no man cometh unto the Father, *but by me.*"
>
> John 14:6

> "I am the door: by *me* if any man enter in, *he shall be saved...* "
>
> John 10:9

Still the Catechism insists:

> "She (Mary) is inseparably linked with the saving work of her Son." Pg. 303, #1172

Once again, it comes down to who you will believe, the Bible or church tradition. The Bible is unmistakably clear:

> "I, even I, am the LORD; and *beside me there is no saviour."* Isaiah 43:11

> "Yet I am the LORD thy God... *there is no saviour beside me."*
>
> Hosea 13:4

> "The God of my rock *he is... my saviour..."* 2 Samuel 22:3

Before Jesus was born, an angel announced that He would be the Savior:

> "And she shall bring forth a son, and thou shalt call his name JESUS: for *he shall save his people from their sins.*"   Matthew 1:21

After Jesus' birth, the angel repeated himself:

> "For unto you is born this day in the city of David *a Saviour, which is Christ the Lord.*"   Luke 2:11

Over and over, we read that Jesus is the Savior:

> "… we have heard him ourselves, and know that this is indeed *the Christ, the Saviour of the world.*" John 4:42

> "Him (Jesus) hath God exalted with his right hand to be a Prince and *a Saviour…*"   Acts 5:31

> "Of this man's seed hath God according to his promise raised unto Israel *a Saviour, Jesus:*"   Acts 13:23

> "But is now made manifest by the appearing of *our Saviour Jesus Christ…*"   2 Timothy 1:10

> "Grace, mercy, and peace, from God the Father and *the Lord Jesus Christ our Saviour.*"   Titus 1:4

> "Which he shed on us abundantly
> through *Jesus Christ our Saviour;*"
> Titus 3:6

> "... the Father sent *the Son* to be *the
> Saviour of the world.*"   1 John 4:14

Look at the words of Peter, recognized as
Catholicism's first pope:

> "... through the righteousness of God
> and *our Saviour Jesus Christ:*"
> 2 Peter 1:1

> "... into the everlasting kingdom of
> *our Lord and Saviour Jesus Christ.*"
> 2 Peter 1:11

> "... through the knowledge of the
> Lord and *Saviour Jesus Christ...*"
> 2 Peter 2:20

Certainly, Peter knew that Jesus, not Mary, was
the Savior. Peter glorified *Jesus* as the Savior, not
Mary:

> "But grow in grace, and in the
> knowledge of our Lord and *Saviour
> Jesus Christ.* To *him* be glory both
> now and for ever. Amen."
> 2 Peter 3:18

This same Peter declares that:

> "... ye were not redeemed with corruptible things, as silver and gold, from your vain conversation received by tradition from your fathers; *But with the precious blood of Christ,* as of a lamb without blemish and without spot:"   1 Peter 1:18-19

Without question, Jesus is the Savior, not Mary.

Conclusion

The facts of this chapter leave several questions needing answers:

• Why does the Catholic church want people looking to Mary instead of Jesus for salvation?

• Why is glory stolen from Jesus and given to Mary?

• If Mary plays a role in salvation, why didn't God tell us so in His Word?

• Most importantly, who will you trust to save you? The Mary of church tradition, or the Jesus of God's Word?

> "For our conversation is in heaven; from whence also we look for *the Saviour, the Lord Jesus Christ:*"
>   Philippians 3:20

16

Mary: Saved from Birth

Catholicism asserts that Mary never sinned and, hence, was redeemed (saved) from the moment of her birth:

> "By the grace of God Mary remained free of every personal sin her whole life long." Pg. 124, #493

> "Espousing the divine will for salvation whole-heartedly, without a single sin to restrain her, she gave herself entirely to the person and to the work of her Son..." Pg. 124, #494

> "Mary is the most excellent fruit of redemption (SC 103): from the first instant of her conception, she was totally preserved from the stain of original sin and she remained pure from all personal sin throughout her life." Pg. 128 #508 (See also Pg. 191, #722)

If you are wondering if this doctrine is taught in God's Word, it isn't. The Catechism admits that it is another church tradition:

> "Through the centuries the Church has become ever more aware that Mary, 'full of grace' through God, was redeemed from the moment of her conception." Pg. 123, #491

But the Bible identifies Jesus as the sinless One, not Mary:

> "For he hath made him (Jesus) to be sin for us, *who knew no sin;* that we might be made the righteousness of God in him."   2 Corinthians 5:21

Aside from the Lord Jesus, the Bible is quite clear that *nobody* else has ever been sinless:

> "For *all have sinned,* and come short of the glory of God;"   Romans 3:23

> "As it is written, There is none righteous, *no, not one:"*   Romans 3:10

> "They are all gone out of the way, they are together become unprofitable; *there is none that doeth good, no, not one."*   Romans 3:12

Notice, none of these verses say "all have sinned, except Mary."

> "But the scripture hath concluded *all* under sin…"   Galatians 3:22

Mary knew she needed a Savior

In Luke's gospel, Mary herself admits that she was a sinner. Otherwise she would never have concluded that she needed a Saviour:

> "And Mary said, My soul doth magnify the Lord, And my spirit hath rejoiced in God *my Saviour."*   Luke 1:46-47

Yet, the Catholic church demands that members worship Mary:

> "The Church's devotion to the Blessed Virgin is intrinsic to Christian worship." Pg. 253, #971

Did Jesus exalt Mary?

Here's how Jesus referred to His mother when Mary asked to see Him one day:

> "Who is my mother? and who are my brethren? And he stretched forth his hand toward his disciples, and said, Behold my mother and my brethren!

> For whosoever shall do the will of my Father which is in heaven, the same is my brother, and sister, and mother."
>   Matthew 12:48-50

Jesus did not say, "Usher in this blessed woman."

Rather, He replied that anyone who obeys God's Word is equal with Mary. Jesus refused to exalt her.

When Others Exalted Mary

When a woman came to Jesus and attempted to exalt Mary, look how the Lord responded:

> "… a certain woman of the company lifted up her voice, and said unto him, Blessed is the womb that bare thee, and the paps which thou hast sucked. But he said, Yea rather, blessed are they that hear the word of God, and keep it." Luke 11:27-28

Jesus announces that those who hear and obey the Word of God are blessed above Mary. Perhaps the Lord inserted these verses for those today who choose to ignore the Word of God so they can follow church traditions.

A Pattern

True to the pattern we have seen throughout this book, Jesus is again robbed of glory and honor that He alone deserves. Rather than recognizing Him as the only sinless One, Catholicism contradicts Scripture and insists that Mary was also sinless. Why?

Conclusion

Was Mary sinless from birth? Catholic tradition wants you to believe she was, but God's Word says she wasn't. Who will you believe?

> "For there is not a just man upon earth, that doeth good, and sinneth not."   Ecclesiastes 7:20

> "Wherefore, as by one man sin entered into the world, and death by sin; and so death passed upon all men, for that *all have sinned:*"   Romans 5:12

17

Mary: Perpetual Virgin

The Catechism records that Mary remained a virgin throughout her entire life:

> "Mary remained a virgin in conceiving her Son, a virgin in giving birth to him, a virgin in carrying him, a virgin in nursing him at her breast, always a virgin." Pg. 128 #510

> "And so the liturgy of the Church celebrates Mary as Aeiparthenos, the 'Ever-virgin.'" Pg. 126, #499

Either Mary remained a virgin or she didn't. The position you will take depends upon who you believe… the traditions of men, or God's Word.

The Bible states that after giving birth to Jesus, Mary bore other children:

> "Is not this the carpenter's son? is not his mother called Mary? **and his brethren,** James, and Joses, and Simon, and Judas?   Matthew 13:55

> "Is not this the carpenter, the son of
> Mary, the ***brother*** of James, and Joses,
> and of Juda, and Simon? and are not
> ***his sisters*** here with us? And they
> were offended at him."   Mark 6:3

The Apostle Paul wrote:

> "But other of the apostles saw I none,
> save James ***the Lord's brother.***"
>   Galatians 1:19

Because these verses so clearly contradict Catholic
doctrine, the Catechism gives this explanation:

> "The Church has always understood these
> passages as not referring to other children of
> the Virgin Mary. In fact James and Joseph,
> 'brothers of Jesus,' are the sons of another
> Mary, a disciple of Christ..." Pg. 126 #500).

Another Mary? Why the twisting of scripture?
These verses clearly refer to Mary, the mother of
Jesus. So why does the Catholic church deliberately
mislead its members?

Is it to propagate an image of Mary as this divine
creature, who is above having a normal marital
relationship with her husband, Joseph?

Is it to make Mary appear more like current
priests and nuns, leading a celibate life?

These are questions you must answer for yourself.

The pagan connection

Why elevate Mary to this "ever-virgin" state? Although it is beyond the scope of this book, there is an amazing resemblance between the Mary of Roman Catholicism and pagan deities that were worshipped in Old Testament times. It should be disconcerting to all Catholics that the Mary of their religion more closely resembles a pagan deity than the Mary of the Bible.

Conclusion

Was Mary this mystical "ever-virgin" or wasn't she? Your choice is again the same. Accept the traditions of men and reject the Word of God. Or believe God's Word as it is written:

> "Thy word is true from the beginning: and every one of thy righteous judgments endureth for ever."
>
> Psalm 119:160

18

Mary: Source of Holiness

The Catechism alleges that the virgin Mary is the model and source of true holiness:

"From the Church he learns the example of holiness and recognizes its model and source in the all-holy Virgin Mary..." Pg. 490, #2030

You will not be surprised to learn that we have another conflict. As we discussed in the previous chapter, the Bible portrays Mary as a sinner who needed a Savior.

Yes, she was blessed to give birth to the Son of God, but that does not make her the source of holiness. Referring to herself, Mary marveled that God had:

"... regarded the low estate of his handmaiden..." Luke 1:48

The Biblical source of holiness

The Bible affirms repeatedly that God is our *only* model of holiness:

> "Who shall not fear thee, O Lord, and glorify thy name? for *thou only art holy:* for all nations shall come and worship before *thee*…"
>
>   Revelation 15:4

> "Exalt ye the LORD our God, and worship at his footstool; *for he is holy.*"   Psalm 99:5

> "Let them praise thy great and terrible name; *for it is holy.*"   Psalm 99:3

Never do we read in Scripture about Mary being holy, much less the source or model of holiness:

> "Exalt the LORD our God, and worship at his holy hill; *for the LORD our God is holy.*"   Psalm 99:9

> "And one cried unto another, and said, Holy, holy, holy, *is the LORD of hosts:* the whole earth is full of *his* glory."   Isaiah 6:3

The words "holy" or "holiness" are used over 600 times in the Bible. Not once does either word refer to Mary.

God announces that we should be holy, as *He* is holy, not as Mary is holy:

> "But as *he which hath called you is holy,* so be ye holy in all manner of conversation; Because it is written, Be ye holy; *for I am holy.*"
>
> 1 Peter 1:15-16

> "For I am the LORD your God: ye shall therefore sanctify yourselves, and ye shall be holy; *for I am holy...*"
>
> Leviticus 11:44

Roman Catholic friend, do you see the difference here? God's Word repeatedly instructs you to look to the eternal God of the universe as your model and source of holiness. Catholicism counters, saying, "No, don't look to God, look to this frail, human woman."

This is nothing short of blasphemy. And we can only ask, "Why does the Catholic church attempt to dethrone God Almighty from His rightful place and set Mary on His throne instead? Why does Catholicism want you looking to Mary for your example of holiness instead of God?

God deserves *all* glory and honor. Plus, He is a jealous God who reminds us that:

"... I will not give my glory unto another."   Isaiah 48:11

Conclusion

Who will be YOUR model of holiness? God Almighty... or a sinful woman? Catholicism demands you look to the woman. The Bible declares that only God is qualified:

> *"Thou art worthy, O Lord,* to receive glory and honour and power: for thou hast created all things, and for thy pleasure they are and were created."
> Revelation 4:11

> *"I am the LORD, your Holy One,* the creator of Israel, your King."
> Isaiah 43:15

19

Mary: The Intercessor

Many faithful Catholics fervently pray to the virgin Mary, believing that she is the mediator who intercedes on their behalf before the Father:

> "Therefore the Blessed Virgin is invoked in the Church under the titles of Advocate, Helper, Benefactress, and Mediatrix." Pg. 252, #969

Here, four specific titles are attributed to Mary. Does she fulfill them? Let's look at each one:

Advocate

The belief that Mary is an advocate before the Father is yet another man-made tradition, not supported by Scripture. Moreover, the Bible defies Catholic doctrine by declaring that Jesus, not Mary, is the only Advocate:

> "…if any man sin, we have an advocate with the Father, *Jesus Christ* the righteous:" 1 John 2:1

Helper

Once again, the Bible disagrees with Catholicism by declaring that Jesus, not Mary, is the only supernatural Helper:

"Behold, ***God is mine helper...***"
                                              Psalm 54:4

"So that we may boldly say, ***The Lord is my helper,*** and I will not fear what man shall do unto me." Hebrews 13:6

"Many are the afflictions of the righteous: but ***the LORD*** delivereth him out of them all."   Psalm 34:19

Never in the Word of God is Mary mentioned as being a supernatural helper.

Benefactress

Here is another tradition of men. The Bible calls no one, including Mary, a "benefactress."

Mediatrix

The Bible never elevates Mary to the position of mediatrix, but it does ordain Jesus as the one and only mediator:

"For there is one God, and one mediator between God and men, ***the man Christ Jesus;***"   1 Timothy 2:5

"And for this cause **he (Christ)** is the mediator of the new testament..."

Hebrews 9:15

Intercessor

The function of both a mediator and an advocate is to intercede on behalf of others. Catholic tradition assigns this position to Mary, whereas God's Word exalts the Lord Jesus Christ as the only intercessor:

"For Christ is not entered into the holy places made with hands... but into heaven itself, **now to appear in the presence of God for us:**"

Hebrews 9:24

"Wherefore he (Jesus) is able also to save them to the uttermost that come unto God by him, seeing he ever liveth **to make intercession for them.**"   Hebrews 7:25

Scripture could not be any plainer about the identity of the true intercessor:

"... **It is Christ** that died, yea rather, that is risen again, who is even at the right hand of God, **who also maketh intercession for us.**"   Romans 8:34

> "... he (Jesus) **maketh intercession** for the saints according to the will of God." Romans 8:27

The Bible reveals that anyone who reaches the Father must go through Jesus Christ:

> "For through **him (Jesus)** we both have access by one Spirit unto the Father." Ephesians 2:18

> "According to the eternal purpose which he purposed in Christ Jesus our Lord: **In whom we have boldness and access..."** Ephesians 3:11-12

Mary is **never** mentioned as an intercessor.

Jesus is degraded again

The Bible is quite definite. Jesus is the only Advocate, Helper, Mediator and Intercessor before the Father. Yet, Catholic tradition strips these four titles away from Him and drops them in Mary's lap instead. Why?

Why is Jesus degraded at every turn? Why is Catholicism determined to take from Jesus everything the Bible attributes to Him and give it to someone or something else?

If Mary is so exalted, why did Bible characters like the Apostle Paul utter words like:

"For I determined not to know any thing among you, *save Jesus Christ,* and him crucified." 1 Corinthians 2:2

Conclusion

Now you know the positions of both the Bible and Catholic tradition. Will you reject the Word of God and give glory to Mary? Or will you reject the traditions of men and give glory to Jesus Christ?:

"But now hath he (Jesus) obtained a more excellent ministry, by how much also *he is the mediator* of a better covenant, which was established upon better promises."   Hebrews 8:6

20

Mary: Recipient of Prayer

Catholic doctrine commands members to pray to the virgin Mary:

> "By asking Mary to pray for us, we acknowledge ourselves to be poor sinners and we address ourselves to the 'Mother of Mercy,' the All-Holy One... May she welcome us as our mother at the hour of our passing to lead us to her son, Jesus, in paradise." Pg. 644, #2677

It is imperative that you know whether these statements are from God or merely traditions of men. Therefore, we will examine each statement:

• *Asking Mary to pray for us:* A tradition of men, not found in the Bible.

• *Mother of Mercy:* Another tradition of men.

• *Mary is the All Holy One:* A tradition of men. We've already shown that God is the only "All Holy One."

• *Mary welcomes us at death:* A tradition of men, not taught in the Bible.

• *Mary leads us to Jesus:* Another tradition of men, not found in God's Word.

Please understand, Catholic friend, God never said *any* of these things. They are all traditions that came from the minds of early Catholic leaders:

> "From the most ancient times the Blessed Virgin has been honored with the title of 'Mother of God,' to whose protection the faithful fly in all their dangers and needs..." Pg. 253, #971

That people should pray to Mary in their times of trouble is another tradition of men concocted by Catholic leaders of the past and handed down to Catholics today. *Never* does Jesus or anyone else in the Bible instruct people to pray to Mary.

Who should we pray to?

The Bible directly contradicts the Catechism by directing people to pray to God alone:

> *"Call unto me,* and I will answer thee, and shew thee great and mighty things, which thou knowest not."
>
> Jeremiah 33:3

> "And *call upon me* in the day of trouble: I will deliver thee, and thou shalt glorify me."   Psalm 50:15

When trouble comes, call upon God, not Mary:

> "Give ear, O Lord, unto my prayer… In the day of my trouble *I will call upon thee:* for thou wilt answer me."
>   Psalm 86:6, 7

> "He shall *call upon me,* and I will answer him: I will be with him in trouble; I will deliver him, and honour him."   Psalm 91:15

Literally hundreds of Scriptures teach us to flee to God when trouble comes our way. Not a single verse encourages us to pray to Mary:

> "But the salvation of the righteous is of the LORD: *he is their strength in the time of trouble.*"   Psalm 37:39

> "O LORD, be gracious unto us; we have waited for thee: be thou their arm every morning, our salvation also *in the time of trouble.*"   Isaiah 33:2

> "Blessed is he that considereth the poor: the LORD will deliver him *in time of trouble.*"   Psalm 41:1

Should you cast your burdens on Mary?

> ***"Cast thy burden upon the LORD,***
> and he shall sustain thee: he shall
> never suffer the righteous to be
> moved."   Psalm 55:22

King David prayed all through the day… to God:

> "Evening, and morning, and at noon,
> will I pray, and cry aloud: and ***he***
> ***shall hear my voice."***   Psalm 55:17

The psalmist proclaimed:

> "The LORD is nigh unto ***all them***
> ***that call upon him,*** to all that call
> upon him in truth."   Psalm 145:18

In the New Testament we read:

> "Be careful for nothing; but in every
> thing by prayer and supplication with
> thanksgiving ***let your requests be***
> ***made known unto God."***
>
>   Philippians 4:6

Who will you pray to?

God's Word says pray to God. Catholicism would
rather have you pray to Mary. Again, one must
wonder why the Catechism demotes Jesus and
exalts Mary. It seems the Catholic church does

not want its members going to Jesus for anything. Yet, Jesus issued this invitation:

> *"Come unto me,* all ye that labour and are heavy laden, and I will give you rest." Matthew 11:28

Either the Bible is wrong, or Catholicism is keeping you away from the One who is ready and willing to meet your every need.

Conclusion

Here is another critical decision you must make. Will you follow the Catholic traditions of men and pray to Mary?

Or will you obey the Holy Scriptures and direct your prayers to God?

> "As for me, *I will call upon God;* and the LORD shall save me."
>
> Psalm 55:16

21

Mary: Queen Over All Things

Catholicism contends that at Mary's death, the Lord took her up into heaven and gave her the title, "Queen over all things:"

"Finally the Immaculate Virgin, preserved free from all stain of original sin, when the course of her earthly life was finished, was taken up body and soul into heavenly glory, and exalted by the Lord as Queen over all things." Pg. 252, #966

Once again, Catholic doctrine and the Word of God have a head-on collision. Scripture not only never teaches such a doctrine, it condemns it. In Jeremiah 44: 9, we read about the worship of a false goddess known as the "Queen of heaven," a practice which made God furious:

"The children gather wood, and the fathers kindle the fire, and the women

> knead their dough, to make cakes to
> the *queen of heaven,* and to pour out
> drink offerings unto other gods, that
> they may *provoke me to anger."*
>
> Jeremiah 7:18

Why did these people worship this false goddess
called the Queen of heaven? It was a tradition of
men that had been handed down to them:

> "But we will… burn incense unto the
> *queen of heaven,* and to pour out
> drink offerings unto her, as we have
> done, we, *and our fathers,* our kings,
> and our princes…"   Jeremiah 44:17

Has Catholicism handed down the same pagan
ritual that infuriates God?

Pagan religions

Although it is beyond the reach of this book,
curious Catholics would be fascinated by a study
of the many false religions which have worshipped
a "Queen of heaven." Given that fact, Catholicism's
insistence that God gave Mary a name so often
used by false goddesses is remarkable.

Who should be exalted?

Though Catholicism insists upon exalting Mary,
the Bible exalts only God Almighty:

*"**Be thou exalted, O God,** above the heavens; let thy glory be above all the earth."*   Psalm 57:5

"... thine is the kingdom, O LORD, and ***thou art exalted*** as head above all."   1 Chronicles 29:11

"... let the God of my salvation ***be exalted.***"   Psalm 18:46

*"**Be thou exalted, LORD,** in thine own strength..."*   Psalm 21:13

"Be still, and know that I am God: ***I will be exalted*** among the heathen, ***I will be exalted*** in the earth."

Psalm 46:10

"... the shields of the earth belong unto God: ***he is greatly exalted.***"

Psalm 47:9

*"**The LORD is exalted;** for he dwelleth on high..."*   Isaiah 33:5

God receives glory through Jesus Christ

The Bible declares that God receives glory through the Lord Jesus Christ. In the New Testament, the name "Jesus" appears 943 times. The name "Christ" appears 533 times, while the words "Lord Jesus" appear 115 times.

The first four books of the New Testament chronicle the birth, life, death and resurrection of Jesus, while the rest of the New Testament revolves around Him.

Mary, on the other hand, appears in God's Word only a handful of times, and is never referred to as a queen of anything:

> "Wherefore **God also hath highly exalted him (Jesus),** and given him a name which is above every name: That at the name of Jesus every knee should bow, of things in heaven, and things in earth, and things under the earth; Philippians 2:9-10

> "... Worthy is the Lamb that was slain (Jesus) to receive power, and riches, and wisdom, and strength, and **honour, and glory,** and blessing." Revelation 5:12

Who should receive all glory? God... through Jesus Christ:

> "... that God in **all things** may be glorified **through Jesus Christ,** to whom be praise and dominion for ever and ever. Amen." 1 Peter 4:11

> "Him (Jesus) ***hath God exalted*** with his right hand to be a Prince and a Saviour, for to give repentance to Israel, and forgiveness of sins."
>
> Acts 5:31

I'm sure you see the pattern again. While the Bible strives to exalt Jesus Christ, Catholicism is determined to demote Jesus and exalt Mary.

Why is Jesus Christ, the One who sacrificed His life and suffered the cruel torture of the cross, set aside and replaced by a mere mortal woman?

Conclusion

Catholicism insists that the Lord elevated Mary to the rank of "Queen of all things." Yet, the Bible proclaims that worshipping a "Queen of heaven" provokes God to anger.

Where will you place your trust, in the traditions of men, or the Word of God?

> "Wherefore God also hath highly exalted him (Jesus), and given him a name which is above ***every*** name..."
>
> Philippians 2:9-11

22

The Mass

If the Catechism is to be believed, then each time the Mass is performed, Christ's work on the cross is made present and the work of our redemption is carried out:

> "In this divine sacrifice which is celebrated in the Mass, the same Christ who offered himself once in a bloody manner on the altar of the cross is contained and is offered in an unbloody manner." Pg. 344, #1367

> "When the Church celebrates the Eucharist, she commemorates Christ's Passover, and it is made present. As often as the sacrifice of the Cross by which Christ our Pasch has been sacrificed is celebrated on the altar, the work of our redemption is carried out." Pg. 343, #1364

But the Bible reveals that the work of redemption was a one time act which was completed when Jesus died on the cross:

> "... but now *once* in the end of the
> world hath he (Jesus) appeared *to put
> away sin* by the sacrifice of himself."
>
> Hebrews 9:26

> "By the which will we are sanctified
> through the offering of the body of
> Jesus Christ *once for all.*"
>
> Hebrews 10:10

When Jesus shed His blood, that one time act
purchased eternal redemption for all who would
put their faith and trust in Christ alone:

> "Neither by the blood of goats and
> calves, but by his own blood he (Jesus)
> entered in *once* into the holy place,
> *having obtained eternal redemption
> for us.*"   Hebrews 9:12

The Bible specifically states that this sacrifice
need *not* be done daily:

> "Who needeth not daily, as those high
> priests, to offer up sacrifice, first for his
> own sins, and then for the people's:
> for this he did *once,* when he offered
> up himself."   Hebrews 7:27

Yet the Catechism is adamant that:

> "Every time this mystery is celebrated, 'the

work of our redemption is carried on'..." Pg. 354, #1405

But God's Word is equally adamant that Christ's death was a one time event:

> "So Christ was *once* offered to bear the sins of many..."   Hebrews 9:28

> "But this man, after he had offered *one sacrifice for sins for ever,* sat down on the right hand of God;"
> Hebrews 10:12

Jesus did all the work necessary to procure man's salvation when He died on the cross. No further work has ever been needed.

Who gets the credit?

For the Catechism to claim that the Catholic church plays a part in the redemptive work of Christ is to steal from the Lord Jesus credit He alone deserves for the work He accomplished at Calvary.

According to God's Word, Christ did it all, once and for all. His death was a divine act, the most wonderful sacrifice ever made. It occurred once, never to be repeated again. Still the Catechism insists:

> "The sacrifice of Christ and the sacrifice of the

Eucharist are one single sacrifice." Pg. 344 #
1367

As lovingly as possible it must be said that this
statement is purely sacrilegious. To suggest that a
priest performing a religious ritual is a part of the
torturous death Jesus endured is nothing short of
blasphemy.

To associate the rituals of the Catholic church
with Christ's work on the cross is ludicrous. The
Catholic church played no part in the work that
made redemption possible and it deserves no
credit.

Once again, Catholicism tries to force Christ to
share His glory with the Catholic church, while
the Bible shows that Jesus alone deserves the glory.

Conclusion

Where will you place your trust? In the Word of
God... or the traditions and teaching of the
Catholic church?

> "For Christ also hath *once* suffered for
> sins, the just for the unjust, that he
> might bring us to God, being put to
> death in the flesh, but quickened by
> the Spirit:"   1 Peter 3:18

23

Purgatory

Catholicism teaches that after death, some people are sent to a place called purgatory for further purification before entering heaven:

> "All who die in God's grace and friendship, but still imperfectly purified, are indeed assured of their eternal salvation; but after death they undergo purification, so as to achieve the holiness necessary to enter the joy of heaven." Pg. 268, #1030

> "The Church gives the name Purgatory to this final purification of the elect..." Pg. 268-269, #1031

Did this critical doctrine come from God, or is it another tradition of men? Here's your answer, right out of the Catechism:

> "The Church formulated her doctrine of faith on Purgatory especially at the Councils of Florence and Trent." Pg. 268-269, #1031

Is it unreasonable to ask where a group of men got their information about the afterlife to formulate such a doctrine?

Precious Roman Catholic, if you are praying for loved ones you believe are in purgatory, you need to be aware that God didn't tell you they were there, a group of religious leaders did:

> "But at the present time some of his disciples are pilgrims on earth. Others have died and are being purified, while still others are in glory..."
> Pg. 249, #954

If you suffer, it's not a gift

What makes this doctrine even more disturbing is that the Bible never indicates such a place exists. Neither does the Bible teach that further purification after death is necessary to earn going to heaven. On the contrary, God's Word declares that salvation is a free gift:

> "For the wages of sin is death; but the **gift of God** is eternal life through Jesus Christ our Lord."   Romans 6:23

> "... by the righteousness of one (Jesus) **the free gift** came upon all men unto justification of life."   Romans 5:18

Would an honest, loving God offer you eternal

life as a free gift—then make you suffer to earn it—then lie about it in His Word?

> "For by grace are ye saved through faith; and that not of yourselves: it is the *gift of God:"* Ephesians 2:8

If the Bible is to be believed, then there is no need for further purification for those who die in Christ. They have already been justified by Jesus:

> "Much more then, being now *justified by his blood,* we shall be saved from wrath through him." Romans 5:9

> "Being *justified freely* by his grace through the redemption that is in Christ Jesus:" Romans 3:24

The Apostle Paul drives home this same point:

> "And such were some of you: but ye are *washed,* but ye are *sanctified,* but ye are *justified* in the name of the Lord Jesus…" 1 Corinthians 6:11

True Christians are already purified because Jesus put away all sin on the cross:

> "… but now once in the end of the world hath he (Jesus) appeared to *put away sin* by the sacrifice of himself."
> Hebrews 9:26

God's children are not required to suffer for salvation because they have been bought and paid for:

> "For ye are **bought with a price:** therefore glorify God in your body, and in your spirit, which are God's."
>   1 Corinthians 6:20

The price was the blood of Jesus Christ:

> "... feed the church of God, which he (Jesus) hath **purchased with his own blood."**   Acts 20:28

Conclusion

If the Bible is so clear on this subject, why did the Catholic church institute a doctrine that has persuaded faithful members to give multiplied millions of dollars to the church to have prayers and Masses said on behalf of departed loved ones? You must answer that for yourself.

Now, at least you know that the doctrine of purgatory was hatched from the minds of mortal men:

> "There is therefore now **no condemnation** to them which are in Christ Jesus, who walk not after the flesh, but after the Spirit."   Romans 8:1

24

Praying to Saints

The Catechism admonishes members to pray to those who, because of their good works, have been declared by the church to be "saints:"

> "The witnesses who have preceded us into the kingdom, especially those whom the Church recognizes as saints, share in the living tradition of prayer by the example of their lives... They contemplate God, praise him and constantly care for those whom they have left on earth. Their intercession is their most exalted service to God's plan. We can and should ask them to intercede for us and for the whole world." Pg. 645, #2683   (See also Pg. 249, #956)

This chapter must begin by defining the word "saint." Catholicism teaches that a saint is one of a select few who, because of good works while alive, is declared a saint after death:

> "By canonizing some of the faithful, i.e., by solemnly proclaiming that they practiced heroic

virtue and lived in fidelity to God's grace, the Church recognizes the power of the Spirit of holiness within her and sustains the hope of believers by proposing the saints to them as models and intercessors." Pg. 219, #828

According to Scripture, however, anyone who is born again by faith in Christ is a saint. Paul wrote to all the saints (Christians) in Rome:

> "To all that be in Rome, beloved of God, ***called to be saints:*** Grace to you and peace from God our Father, and the Lord Jesus Christ."   Romans 1:7

Many other verses express the same truth:

> "Unto me, who am less than the least of ***all saints,*** is this grace given, that I should preach among the Gentiles the unsearchable riches of Christ;"
> Ephesians 3:8

> "… Behold, the Lord cometh with ***ten thousands of his saints,***" Jude 1:14

> "And he gave some, apostles; and some, prophets; and some, evangelists; and some, pastors and teachers; ***For the perfecting of the saints,*** for the work of the ministry, for the edifying of ***the body of Christ:***"   Ephesians 4:11-12

(See also Acts 9:13; 9:32; 9:41; 26:10; Romans 8:27; 12:13; 15:25; 15:26; 15:31; 16:2; 16:15; 1 Corinthians 6:1, 2 Corinthians 1:1, Ephesians 1:1, plus dozens of other New Testament references.)

Why this doctrine?

In short, the scenario goes like this. Catholicism discarded the scriptural definition of a "saint" and devised a new one, then instructed members to pray to these unscriptural "saints."

The question is, why pray to anyone else when the God of the universe is in heaven waiting to hear and answer prayers?

Are "saints" intercessors?

Supposedly, these so-called saints "intercede with the Father for us." But we have already learned that Jesus Christ is our *only* intercessor. Therefore, to suggest otherwise is but a man made tradition.

Here's another interesting Catechism quote concerning saints:

> "Exactly as Christian communion among our fellow pilgrims brings us closer to Christ, so our communion with the saints joins us to Christ..." Pg. 249-250, #957

According to the Catholic church, praying to saints brings people closer to Christ. However, you will not find this doctrine in Scripture either. It is another tradition of men that neither Jesus nor the Bible ever taught.

In fact, this practice of communing with the dead treads dangerously close to necromancy, another practice strongly condemned in the Bible. (See Deuteronomy 18:10-12.)

Conclusion

The nagging question you must answer here is: Why would the Catholic church rather have members pray to dead men than to the living, all-powerful, prayer-answering God?

Keep in mind that if these traditions of men are not true, then all your prayers to "saints" are but worthless chatter.

If you pray to God, though, you may claim many wonderful Biblical promises:

> "Let us therefore come boldly unto the throne of grace, that we may obtain mercy, and find grace to help in time of need."   Hebrews 4:16

25

Praying For The Dead

Can the living help the dead by praying for them? According to Catholic doctrine, they can:

> *"Communion with the dead.* In full consciousness of this communication of the whole Mystical Body of Jesus Christ, the Church in its pilgrim members, from the earliest days of the Christian religion, has honored with great respect the memory of the dead; and because it is a holy and wholesome thought to pray for the dead that they may be loosed from their sins she offers her suffrages for them. Our prayer for them is capable not only of helping them, but also of making their intercession for us effective." Pg. 250, #958

Three statements here contradict the Bible. Let's look at each:

1. *"It is a holy and wholesome thought to pray for the dead."*

According to God's Word, it is neither holy nor wholesome to pray for the dead. Christians are instructed to pray for the living, but not one example exists of true Christians praying for the dead. This is another tradition of men.

2. *Praying for the dead can help loose them from their sins.*

Here is a tradition built upon a tradition. The Scriptures never suggest that this statement is true. As we have already learned, one must be loosed from their sins **before** death.

3. *Our prayers make their intercession for us effective.*

Like building blocks, they keep piling, tradition on top of tradition, all without any scriptural foundation. Now, we have reached a peak, where our prayers are supposedly capable of:

"... making their intercession for us effective."

The obvious question is: Why do we need others interceding for us? Isn't it enough to have God the Son interceding for us? Does the Creator of the Universe need the help of mortal men and women to persuade the Father on our behalf?

What a degrading attitude towards Jesus Christ. The Catholic position insults the Lord by portraying Him as an incapable, powerless bystander who needs the help of anyone He can grab to persuade the Father. This is not the picture of Jesus presented in the Bible. Jesus declared of Himself:

> "... *All power* is given unto me in heaven and in earth." Matthew 28:18

Here's another Biblical portrait of Jesus Christ:

> "Which he (God) wrought in Christ, when he raised him from the dead, and set him at his own right hand in the heavenly places, *Far above all principality, and power, and might, and dominion,* and every name that is named, not only in this world, but also in that which is to come: And hath put *all things* under his feet, and gave him to be the head over *all things* to the church,"
>
> Ephesians 1:20-22

How different this is from the Catholic picture of Jesus, which reduces the Lord to a spiritual weakling devoid of power and authority. Dear Catholic friend, Jesus Christ does not need help from *anyone!* He is well able to do the job:

> "Wherefore he (Jesus) is able also to save them to the uttermost that come unto God by him, seeing *he ever liveth to make intercession for them.*"
>
> Hebrews 7:25

Before you pray for another deceased loved one, please understand that these are all man-made rules. God never asked you to pray for the dead, nor did He promised it would do any good.

As a young Catholic, I always assumed that all these rules were somehow coming from God. But they're not! Read the Bible and see for yourself. The Catechism teaches traditions of men, not commands of God.

The Same Pattern

Surely, you have noticed that Jesus has taken yet another serious demotion. From the One and only Divine Intercessor at the Father's right hand, Jesus is hurled down into the crowd of dead humans and is relegated to being one of many intercessors. Why does the Catholic religion keep doing this to the Lord Jesus Christ?

Conclusion

Once again, you are faced with several important decisions:

• Will you continue praying for the dead, knowing that it is a tradition of men and not a command of God?

• Will you cling to a doctrine which degrades the Lord Jesus Christ so that church tradition can be exalted?

• Will you knowingly reject the Word of God to follow man's traditions?

These are decisions you must make. As you ponder these things, remember the words of Jesus:

> "But in vain they do worship me, teaching for doctrines the commandments of men."   Matthew 15:9

26

Statues

The Catechism requires all Catholics to "venerate" statues, or images of Christ, Mary and others:

> "Sacred images in our churches and homes are intended to awaken and nourish our faith in the mystery of Christ. Through the icon of Christ and his works of salvation, it is he whom we adore. Through sacred salvation, it is he whom we adore. Through sacred images of the holy Mother of God, of the angels and of the saints, we venerate the persons represented." Pg. 307, #1192

Regardless of what statues are intended to do, one thing is certain—they transgress God's instructions. When God gave the ten commandments, the second one was:

> "Thou shalt not make unto thee *any graven image,* or any likeness of any thing that is in heaven above, or that

is in the earth beneath, or that is in the water under the earth:"

Exodus 20:4

God also ordered:

"Neither shalt thou set thee up any image; *which the LORD thy God hateth.*" Deuteronomy 16:22

The Bible concludes that those who make or have statues have been corrupted:

"Take ye therefore good heed unto yourselves... Lest ye corrupt yourselves, and make you a graven image, the similitude of any figure, the likeness of male or female..."

Deuteronomy 4:15-16

God states His position again:

"Take heed unto yourselves, lest ye forget the covenant of the LORD your God, which he made with you, and make you a graven image, or the likeness of any thing, which the LORD thy God hath forbidden thee."

Deuteronomy 4:23

God's Word also expressly forbids people from bowing down to statues, which is customary in the Catholic church. Whenever you see a picture of the pope bowing before a statue of Mary, you should think about this verse of Holy Scripture:

> "Thou shalt **not bow down thyself to them,** nor serve them: for I the LORD thy God am a jealous God..."
>
> Exodus 20:5

In the New Testament, the Apostle Paul explains why God was so adamant about idols:

> "What say I then? that the idol is any thing, or that which is offered in sacrifice to idols is any thing?... the things which the Gentiles sacrifice, they sacrifice **to devils (demons)**, and not to God: and I would not that ye should have fellowship with devils."
>
> 1 Corinthians 10:19-20

Behind every idol is a literal demon, and God does not want anyone fellowshipping with demons. No wonder God forbids the use of idols:

> **"Turn ye not unto idols,** nor make to yourselves molten gods: I am the LORD your God." Leviticus 19:4

God hates idolatry:

> "But now I have written unto you not

> to keep company, if any man that is called a brother be a fornicator, or covetous, ***or an idolater...*** with such an one no not to eat."
>
> 1 Corinthians 5:11

> "For this ye know, that no whore-monger, nor unclean person, nor covetous man, who is ***an idolater,*** hath any inheritance in the kingdom of Christ and of God." Ephesians 5:5

Here, God declares that idolaters will not enter heaven. The next verses warns:

> ***"Let no man deceive you with vain words:*** for because of these things cometh the wrath of God upon the children of disobedience."
>
> Ephesians 5:6

Is the Catholic church deceiving ***you*** with vain words? You must decide that for yourself.

Origin of this doctrine

Catholicism does not even pretend that this doctrine came from God:

> "Following the divinely inspired teaching of our holy Fathers and the tradition of the Catholic Church (for we know that this tradition comes from the Holy Spirit who dwells

in her) we rightly define with full certainty and correctness that, like the figure of the precious and life-giving cross, venerable and holy images of our Lord and God and Savior, Jesus Christ, our inviolate Lady, the holy Mother of God, and the venerated angels, all the saints and the just, whether painted or made of mosaic or another suitable material, are to be exhibited in the holy churches of God, on sacred vessels and vestments, walls and panels, in houses and on streets." Pg. 300, #1161

This doctrine came from the "holy Fathers" and "tradition of the Catholic Church." You are expected to believe that these holy Fathers were "divinely inspired" to violate God's Word. Can you accept this?

The psalmist teaches us even more on the subject:

> "The idols of the heathen are silver and gold, the work of men's hands. They have mouths, but they speak not; eyes have they, but they see not; They have ears, but they hear not; neither is there any breath in their mouths. They that make them are like unto them: so is every one that trusteth in them."   Psalm 135:15-18

In other words, as an idol is deaf and dumb, so

everyone who makes idols or trusts in them is devoid of understanding.

This is a powerful warning from a loving and compassionate God.

Conclusion

The Catholic church contends that idols will "awaken and nourish" your faith in "the mystery of Christ." But God's Word forbids their use. Who will you obey?

> "Ye shall make you no idols nor graven image, neither rear you up a standing image, neither shall ye set up any image of stone in your land, to bow down unto it: for I am the LORD your God."   Leviticus 26:1

> "For laying aside the commandment of God, ye hold the tradition of men..."   Mark 7:8

27

Confirmation

Confirmation, besides being one of the sacraments necessary for salvation, also provides Catholics with other benefits, says the Catechism:

"Confirmation perfects Baptismal grace; it is the sacrament which gives the Holy Spirit in order to root us more deeply in the divine filiation, incorporate us more firmly into Christ, strengthen our bond with the Church..." Pg. 333, #1316

Supposedly, Confirmation incorporates Catholics more *firmly* into Christ. But the Bible teaches no such doctrine. According to God's Word, you are either in Christ or you are not. Being more firmly incorporated into Christ is never taught:

"Therefore if any man be *in Christ*, he is a new creature: old things are passed away; behold, all things are become new." 2 Corinthians 5:17

Once you are born into God's family, there is no person or thing that can remove you from it:

> "For I am persuaded, that neither death, nor life, nor angels, nor principalities, nor powers, nor things present, nor things to come, Nor height, nor depth, nor any other creature, shall be able to separate us from the love of God, which is *in Christ Jesus* our Lord."
>
> Romans 8:38-39

A child of God does not need to be more firmly incorporated into Christ:

> "There is therefore now no condemnation to them which are *in Christ Jesus,* who walk not after the flesh, but after the Spirit."   Romans 8:1

> "But now *in Christ Jesus* ye who sometimes were far off are made nigh by the blood of Christ."
>
> Ephesians 2:13

A spiritual imprint?

Another supposed benefit of Confirmation is that:

> "Confirmation, like Baptism, imprints a spiritual mark or indelible character on the Christian's soul…" Pg. 333, #1317

You can search the Bible, but you will not read about the imprinting of spiritual marks on a Christian's souls. The Catechism tells us why:

> "The imposition of hands is rightly recognized by the **Catholic tradition** as the origin of the sacrament of Confirmation..." Pg. 326 #1288

Confirmation is not in the Bible because it's a tradition of men... a life-long tradition that is to be performed up until the last moment of a Catholic's life:

> "If a Christian is in danger of death, any priest should give him Confirmation. Indeed, the Church desires that none of her children, even the youngest, should depart this world without having been perfected by the Holy Spirit with the gift of Christ's fullness." Pg. 332, #1314

The real purpose of Confirmation

The practical result is that this ritual brings people into deeper bondage to the Catholic church. Surprisingly, the Catechism admits this:

> "For by the sacrament of Confirmation, [the baptized] are more perfectly **bound to the Church...**" Pg. 326 #1285

But why would anyone need or want to be bound to the rules of the Catholic church, considering that Jesus came to set people free?

"If the Son therefore shall make you free, ye shall be *free indeed.*"

John 8:36

"Stand fast therefore in the liberty wherewith *Christ hath made us free...*" Galatians 5:1

Conclusion

Is the man-made Roman Catholic tradition of Confirmation necessary for salvation?

• God's Holy Word emphatically states, "No!"

• The Catholic church disregards the Bible and insists that it is.

Who will you believe... the Word of God, or the commandments of men?

"But in vain they do worship me, teaching for doctrines the commandments of men." Matthew 15:9

28

Confessing Sins to a Priest

Regarding the forgiveness of sins, two critical doctrines must be examined. First, all sins must be confessed to a priest:

> "One who desires to obtain reconciliation with God and with the Church, must confess to a priest all the unconfessed grave sins he remembers after having carefully examined his conscience." Pg. 374, #1493

> "Confession to a priest is an essential part of the sacrament of Penance:" Pg. 365, #1456

> "It is called the sacrament of confession, since the disclosure or confession of sins to a priest is an essential element of this sacrament. Pg. 357, #1424 (See also Pg. 374, #1493).

Catholicism orders members to confess their sins to a man, but the Bible reveals that those who

have been born into God's family can go straight to
God's throne to receive forgiveness for their sins:

> "I acknowledged my sin **unto thee,**
> and mine iniquity have I not hid. I
> said, I will confess my transgressions
> **unto the LORD;** and thou forgavest
> the iniquity of my sin. "   Psalm 32:5

> "If we confess our sins, he is faithful
> and just to forgive us our sins, and to
> cleanse us from all unrighteousness."
> 1 John 1:9

David confessed his sins to God when he prayed:

> "Wash me throughly from mine iniq-
> uity, and cleanse me from my sin. For
> I acknowledge my transgressions: and
> my sin is ever before me."
> Psalm 51:2-3

Here is why true Christians have access to God's
throne:

> "Having therefore, brethren, boldness
> to enter into the holiest **by the blood
> of Jesus..."**   Hebrews 10:19

Because of the sinless blood that Jesus Christ shed
on the cross, we have the authority to go straight
to the throne of God for forgiveness.

The "first pope's" example

In the book of Acts, a man named Simon came to the alleged first pope, Peter, wanting to buy the power of the Holy Spirit. How did Peter respond to this sin? Did he suggest that Simon make a confession to him right there? No, Peter told him to repent and confess his sin to God and ask God to forgive him. (See Acts 8:18-22).

Can priests forgive sins?

The second part of this doctrine suggests that Catholic priests have the power to forgive sins:

> "Only priests who have received the faculty of absolving from the authority of the Church can forgive sins in the name of Christ." Pg. 374, #1495 (See also Pg. 364 #1448)

Here, too, Catholic doctrine opposes God's Word:

> "Why doth this man thus speak blasphemies? who can forgive sins **but God only?"**   Mark 2:7

Catholicism teaches that the priest is a mediator between God and man. (See Pg. 365, #1456). But the Bible recognizes only one mediator:

> "For there is one God, and one mediator between God and men, **the man Christ Jesus;"**   1 Timothy 2:5

Once again, the Catechism admits that these are not instructions from God, but traditions of men:

> "The *Fathers of the Church* present this sacrament as the second plank [of salvation]…"
> Pg. 363 #1446

More bondage

> "According to the Church's command, 'after having attained the age of discretion, each of the faithful is *bound* by an obligation faithfully to confess serious sins at least once a year.'" Pg. 365, #1457 *(Emphasis author's)*

There is that word "bound" again. The Church Fathers created another tradition which keeps people in bondage to the Catholic church.

What a powerful weapon to use against Catholics around the world. In essence, this doctrine proclaims that if you leave the Catholic church, you cannot obtain forgiveness for your sins, which means you won't go to heaven.

Please remember, none of this came from God! These are all man-made threats. May God open your spiritual eyes and give you understanding, so that you may see the depth of the bondage this religion holds you in. May God show you that you don't have to be held captive to this religion any longer. Jesus Christ wants to set you free.

Conclusion

Millions of faithful Catholics blindly file into confessional booths, believing that the priest has the power to forgive their sins.

What about you? Where will *you* go to have your sins forgiven? To a sinful priest, as the man-made traditions of the Catholic church demand?

Or will you go straight to God Almighty, as the Bible teaches?

> "Out of the depths have *I cried unto thee, O LORD.* Lord, hear my voice: let thine ears be attentive to the voice of my supplications. If thou, LORD, shouldest mark iniquities, O Lord, who shall stand? But there is forgiveness *with thee,* that thou mayest be feared."　　　　Psalm 130:1-4

29

Indulgences

Through indulgences, the sins of Roman Catholics, both those who are alive and those in Purgatory, can supposedly be forgiven:

> "Through indulgences the faithful can obtain the remission of temporal punishment resulting from sin for themselves and also for the souls in Purgatory." Pg. 374, #1498

Here is the Catechism's definition of an indulgence:

> "An indulgence is a remission before God of the temporal punishment due to sins whose guilt has already been forgiven, which the faithful Christian who is duly disposed gains under certain prescribed conditions through the action of the Church which, as the minister of redemption, dispenses and applies with authority the treasury of the satisfactions of Christ and the saints." Pg. 370, #1471

Here, the water gets deep. Space does not permit a full explanation of indulgences. Suffice it to say that they are a complicated system of good works. It should also be mentioned that every rule regarding indulgences is a tradition of men. Not one can be found in God's Word.

Categories of sins?

"To understand this doctrine (Indulgences) and practice of the Church, it is necessary to understand that sin has a double consequence." Pg. 370, #1472

But the Bible consistently reveals that all sin has the same consequence:

"For the wages of ***sin is death...***"
Romans 6:23

"Then when lust hath conceived, it bringeth forth sin: and ***sin,*** when it is finished, ***bringeth forth death.***"
James 1:15

The final result of sin is always death, no matter how minor we may think a particular sin is. Catholics try to pay for sins through indulgences, but Christ already paid for ***every*** sin:

"For I delivered unto you first of all that which I also received, how that ***Christ died for our sins*** according to the scriptures;"   1 Corinthians 15:3

While it is true that God does want His children to perform good works, those works are not a requirement for salvation, they are a result of salvation. Paul teaches:

> "For by *grace are ye saved* through faith; and that not of yourselves: it is the gift of God: Not of works, lest any man should boast. For we are his workmanship, created in Christ Jesus *unto good works,* which God hath before ordained that we should walk in them."   Ephesians 2:8, 10

Once one is saved by grace, good works should follow. But good works are *never* a requirement for salvation. Neither are they a requirement for forgiveness of sins after salvation.

The New Testament bulges with examples of Jesus forgiving sins, but He never demanded good works as a condition of forgiveness.

Can the living help the dead?

Catholicism also purports that indulgences help those who have already died:

> "Since the faithful departed now being purified are also members of the same communion of saints, one way we can help them is to obtain indulgences for them, so that the temporal pun-

ishments due for their sins may be re-mitted."
Pg. 371-372, #1479

Here is another load of man-made traditions. You will never find any of this taught in the Word of God. As we have mentioned previously, the time to have your sins remitted is while you are still alive.

Three themes

In this doctrine, three recurring themes come to the surface again:

1. Another divine attribute of Jesus is minimized. The Bible declares that only Christ's work can bring about the forgiveness of sins. Catholicism, though, claims that sins can be forgiven through the good works of any ordinary Catholic.

2. Indulgences keep people in bondage to the Catholic church. Rather than going to God for forgiveness, Catholics must toil and strive, performing good deeds through the Catholic church for forgiveness of their sins.

It is noteworthy to ponder that the "good works" of Catholicism differ from the good works of the Bible. Biblical good works are deeds done for other people, while Catholicism's good works revolve primarily around performing rituals of the church (Masses, saying rosaries, Catholic prayers, lighting candles, etc.). God intended good works to benefit others, not to bring people into bondage to a church.

3. Indulgences are a form of spiritual blackmail, forcing members to remain faithful to the church, so they can someday help their loved ones reach heaven.

Conclusion

Is this system of good works from God? Read what God records in His Holy Word on the subject, then decide for yourself:

> "Not by works of righteousness which we have done, but according to his mercy he saved us..." Titus 3:5

30

Interpreting God's Word

Are Catholics able to interpret God's Word for themselves?

> "The task of interpreting the Word of God authentically has been entrusted solely to the magisterium of the Church, that is, to the Pope and to the bishops in communion with him."
> Pg. 30, #100

Can **only** the pope and the leadership of the Catholic church properly interpret God's Word? Let's go to the Bible and see how God feels about this teaching. When Paul and Silas preached in Berea, the people:

> "… received the word with all readiness of mind, and **searched the scriptures** daily, whether those things were so."
> Acts 17:11

In other words, they interpreted the Scriptures for themselves with the help of the Holy Spirit.

> "And Jesus answering said unto them,
> Do ye not therefore err, because ye
> know not the scriptures, neither the
> power of God?"   Mark 12:24

Why did Jesus chastise the Sadducees for not knowing the Scriptures if it was impossible for them to interpret them?

And why did Peter, Catholicism's first "pope," declare the following?

> "Knowing this first, that no prophecy
> of the scripture is of any ***private
> interpretation.***"   2 Peter 1:20

Why does Paul instruct us to study the Bible if we can't interpret it?

> "***Study*** to shew thyself approved unto
> God, a workman that needeth not to
> be ashamed, ***rightly dividing the
> word of truth.***"   2 Timothy 2:15

Jesus admonished the Jews to:

> ***"Search the scriptures..."*** John 5:39

Why would He do that, if He knew they couldn't interpret them?

Who does the interpreting?

The Bible reveals that the Holy Spirit, not a

group of men, will interpret Scripture for God's children and will help them understand all things:

> "But the Comforter, which is the Holy Ghost, whom the Father will send in my name, *he shall teach you all things,* and bring all things to your remembrance, whatsoever I have said unto you."   John 14:26

> "Howbeit when he, the Spirit of truth, is come, *he will guide you into all truth..."*   John 16:13

The Apostle Paul recognized that the Holy Spirit was the One who taught him:

> "Which things also we speak, not in the words which man's wisdom teacheth, but which *the Holy Ghost teacheth;* comparing spiritual things with spiritual."   1 Corinthians 2:13

> "Now we have received, not the spirit of the world, but *the spirit which is of God;* that we might know the things that are freely given to us of God."   1 Corinthians 2:12

Why are Christians commanded to memorize the Scriptures if they can't understand them?

"Thy word have I hid in mine heart, that I might not sin against thee."

Psalm 119:11

"Keep my commandments, and live... write them upon the table of thine heart." Proverbs 7:2-3

A warning

The following verses of Scripture should alarm anyone who believes they need a church to interpret the Bible for them:

"These things have I written unto you concerning them that *seduce you.* But the anointing which ye have received of him abideth in you, and *ye need not that any man teach you:* but as the same anointing teacheth you of all things, and is truth, and is no lie, and even as it hath taught you, ye shall abide in him." 1 John 2:26-27

Could God's position be any plainer?

Conclusion

Why is the Catholic church so determined to interpret the Scriptures for you? Is it because they want to control you and keep you in bondage to Catholicism?

Are they afraid that if you read the Scriptures for yourself, you might discover that Catholic doctrines are contrary to God's Word?

Do you really believe that all non-Catholics are groping around in spiritual blindness, needing the Catholic church to interpret the Bible for them?

You must settle these things in your own mind, but your most important decision is:

> "Who will interpret Scripture for you... the Holy Spirit of God or the Roman Catholic church?"

Your answer to that question will determine who you will obey and eventually where you will spend eternity:

> "O how love I thy law! it is my meditation all the day. Thou through thy commandments hast made me wiser than mine enemies: for they are ever with me. I have more understanding than all my teachers: for thy testimonies are my meditation."
>
> Psalm 119:97-99

31

Catholic Prayer

"Prayer cannot be reduced to the spontaneous outpouring of interior impulse: in order to pray, one must have the will to pray. Nor is it enough to know what the Scriptures reveal about prayer: one must also learn how to pray. Through a living transmission (Sacred Tradition) within 'the believing and praying Church,' the Holy Spirit teaches the children how to pray." Pg. 637, #2650

This Catechism quote makes two remarkably controversial statements. Let's look at each. First:

"Prayer cannot be reduced to the spontaneous outpouring of interior impulse:"

According to the Bible, *it can!* God's Word contains thousands of examples of spontaneous outpourings... and God heard every one of them:

"I cried unto the LORD with my voice, *and he heard me...*" Psalm 3:4

> "O LORD my God, I cried unto
> thee, ***and thou hast healed me.***"
>
>   Psalm 30:2

> "In my distress I cried unto the
> LORD, ***and he heard me.***"
>
>   Psalm 120:1

> "Trust in him at all times; ye people,
> ***pour out your heart before him:*** God
> is a refuge for us. Selah."   Psalm 62:8

Rather than spontaneous outpourings, Catholic
prayers are an endless repetition of written words.
Interestingly, Jesus forbids this method of praying,
claiming it is a practice the "heathen" perform:

> "But when ye pray, ***use not vain
> repetitions,*** as the heathen do: for
> they think that they shall be heard for
> their much speaking."   Matthew 6:7

Secondly, the Catechism contends:

> "Nor is it enough to know what the Scriptures
> reveal about prayer: one must also learn how to
> pray. Through a living transmission (Sacred
> Tradition) within 'the believing and praying
> Church,' the Holy Spirit teaches the children
> how to pray.'"

Here, the Catechism proclaims that the Scriptures
can't teach you how to pray. For that you must

have the Catholic church. However, long before there was a Catholic church, people prayed and received answers to their prayers:

> "Abraham prayed unto God: and *God healed Abimelech, and his wife, and his maidservants…"* Genesis 20:17

> "… when Moses prayed unto the LORD, *the fire was quenched."*
> Numbers 11:2

> "Elisha prayed unto the LORD, and said, Smite this people, I pray thee, with blindness. And *he smote them with blindness according to the word of Elisha."* 2 Kings 6:18

These people spontaneously poured out their hearts to God, without help from the Catholic church. God offers His children this invitation:

> "And *call upon me* in the day of trouble: I will deliver thee, and thou shalt glorify me." Psalm 50:15

> "Be careful for nothing; but in every thing by prayer and supplication with thanksgiving *let your requests be made known unto God."*
> Philippians 4:6-7

God's Word teaches that God not only accepts spontaneous outpourings, He encourages them.

Bondage?

Is it a coincidence that this Catholic doctrine further wraps members in bondage to the Catholic church? That is for you to decide.

Conclusion

We have a standoff. The Bible condemns Catholicism's form of prayer, and the Catholic church condemns the Biblical form of prayer. Obviously, you must choose sides.

Will you side with God and His Holy Word, or with the traditions of men?

> "They cried unto thee, and were delivered: they trusted in thee, and were not confounded."   Psalm 22:5

32

Penance

Another series of good works which Catholicism requires is known as penance:

> "Absolution takes away sin, but it does not remedy all the disorders sin has caused. Raised up from sin, the sinner must still recover his full spiritual health by doing something more to make amends for the sin: he must 'make satisfaction for' or 'expiate' his sins. This satisfaction is also called 'penance.'" Pg. 366, #1459

Millions of Catholics around the world faithfully perform penance, believing these good works are required by God to "make amends for" their sins and to restore them to "full spiritual health."

However, the written Scriptures reveal that this practice is another tradition of men that defies God's Word and degrades the work Christ did on the cross.

175

As we have already covered, Christ paid the full price for our sins at Calvary. To believe that good works are necessary to recover one's "full spiritual health" is to deny God's Word. God makes this promise to all who put their faith in Jesus Christ:

> "And their sins and iniquities will I remember no more. Now where remission of these is, there is no more offering for sin."   Hebrews 10:17-18

God promises **never** to remember the sins of true Christians, and declares that once sins are forgiven through faith in Christ, there is no more offering for sin. In other words, there aren't any works you can do that will cause your sins to be forgiven. Christ did it all!

Yet, the Catechism keeps pouring out man-made rules:

> "The penance the confessor imposes must take into account the penitent's personal situation and must seek his spiritual good. It must correspond as far as possible with the gravity and nature of the sins committed." Pg 367, #1460

The Catechism even defines specific good works that can constitute penance:

> "(Penance) can consist of prayer, an offering, works of mercy, service of neighbor, voluntary

self-denial, sacrifices, and above all the patient acceptance of the cross we must bear." Pg 367, #1460

But God has never demanded good works for forgiveness of sins:

> "For thou, Lord, art good, and ready
> to forgive; and plenteous in mercy
> unto all them that *call upon thee.*"
>
> Psalm 86:5

The Bible declares that Christians are justified through Jesus Christ, not good works:

> "Knowing that a man is not justified
> by the works of the law, but *by the
> faith of Jesus Christ...* for by the
> works of the law shall *no flesh be
> justified.*"   Galatians 2:16

Paul knew that if righteousness was earned through good works, then Christ died for nothing:

> "I do not frustrate the grace of God:
> for if righteousness come by the law,
> then Christ is dead in vain."
>
> Galatians 2:21

The Catechism even extends this tradition to suggest that penance can help the dead:

> "The Church also commends almsgiving,

indulgences, and works of penance undertaken on behalf of the dead:" Pg. 269, #1032

Like cement blocks on a concrete wall, they keep piling, tradition on top of tradition. And every one violates clear teachings of Scripture.

Three Questions

This Catholic doctrine raises at least three more questions you must answer for yourself:

• Is it a coincidence that this unbiblical doctrine keeps people in bondage to the Catholic church?

• Why does Catholicism again demote Jesus Christ by insisting that His sacrifice was not sufficient, and that Catholics must add their own sacrifice to pay for sins?

• Lastly, and most importantly, who will you side with on this issue?… the traditions of men, or the Word of God?

> "Therefore we conclude that a man is justified by faith *without the deeds of the law.*"   Romans 3:28

33

Are Catholics Christ?

"Let us rejoice then and give thanks that we have become not only Christians, but Christ himself. Marvel and rejoice: we have become Christ." Pg. 210, #795

Wow! Notice that Catholics are not merely Christians, they have become "Christ himself."

"My church cannot possibly teach this," Catholics often argue. But two additional catechism quotes further prove this is official Catholic doctrine.

"For the Son of man became man so that we might become God." Pg. 116, #460

"The only-begotten Son of God, wanting to make us sharers in his divinity, assumed our nature, so that he, made man, might make men gods." Pg. 116, #460

Even nominal Catholics know this is utter nonsense. So the million dollar question is, "What are these quotes doing in the book of official Roman Catholic doctrine?

According to Jesus Christ, all who claim to be Christ are deceivers:

> "For many shall come in my name, saying, I am Christ; and shall **deceive many.**"   Matthew 24:5

Jesus warned about being taken in by these deceivers:

> "Take heed that ye **be not deceived:** for many shall come in my name, saying, I am Christ..."   Luke 21:8

> "Then if any man shall say unto you, Lo, here is Christ, or there; **believe it not.**"   Matthew 24:23

Yet the question remains. If the Catholic church does not believe this, then why are these quotes in the catechism?

Many Catholics have written me, asking "How could you write such a thing? We don't believe that." But I did not write the catechism. I only quoted it. And they never answer the question, "If your religion does not believe these doctrines, why are they in your book of official doctrine?"

Some Catholics accuse me of twisting the words. If you feel this way, please go back and read the quotes again. They are direct, easy-to-understand statements. It is impossible to twist them. So the question remains, "Why are the quotes there?"

At least false cults like Mormonism and occultic New Agers admit teaching this unbiblical doctrine. They completely reject Bible verses like:

> "... I am God, and *there is none else;* I am God, and *there is none like me,"* Isaiah 46:9

Roman Catholicism also rejects such verses, for there is only one answer to the question at hand. These quotes appear in the catechism for one simple reason... because they are official Roman Catholic doctrine.

The ultimate insult

Throughout this book, you have seen how Catholic doctrines steal honor and glory due to Jesus Christ and give it to Mary, popes, wafers, saints, statues, etc. But this is the ultimate insult.

The Creator of the universe, the King of kings and Lord of lords, has been dethroned and declared no better than any Catholic on the street.

Where could such an ungodly doctrine come from? Remember how Satan boasted that he would exalt his throne "above the stars of God"

(Isaiah 14:13)? This same Satan declared "I will be like the most High" (Isaiah 14:14). The devil has always longed to be like God. Is this doctrine a clue as to the real father of Roman Catholicism?

Was it not Satan who deceived Adam and Eve, promising they would be "as gods" if they ate of the forbidden fruit (Genesis 3:5)?

Is Satan still using this same lie to deceive Roman Catholics, promising you that, simply by being a Catholic, you can become God Himself?

You should be outraged that an official Catholic doctrine reflects the desires and goals of Satan, and rejects the teachings of God's Word.

Conclusion

Here is the next question you must answer: "Am I willing to remain in a church that openly teaches outright satanic heresy?"

> "But to us there is but one God, the Father, of whom are all things, and we in him; and *one Lord Jesus Christ,* by whom are all things, and we by him."   1 Corinthians 8:6

34

Could 850 Million Catholics be Wrong?

The Catechism pronounces that, as the one true church, those who are baptized into the Catholic church are assured of heaven:

> "The Church does not know of any other means other than Baptism that assures entry into eternal beatitude..." Pg. 320, #1257

In the United States, that means 25 percent of the population, or over 60 million people, are headed for heaven.

In many other countries, ninety percent or more of the population is Catholic, meaning nine out of every ten people will pass through the pearly gates. Worldwide, Catholicism claims nearly one billion members.

You may not believe that nearly a billion people could be wrong, but look what Jesus said:

> "Enter ye in at the strait gate: for wide
> is the gate, and broad is the way, that
> leadeth to ***destruction,*** and ***many***
> there be which go in thereat: Because
> strait is the gate, and narrow is the way,
> which leadeth unto life, and ***few*** there
> be that find it."   Matthew 7:13-14

According to Jesus, the masses willingly accept
false religious systems that lead to destruction,
while few find true salvation that leads to heaven.
Could 60 million Americans be considered "few?"
Would anyone say that one billion people worldwide is a "few?"

When Jesus walked the earth, a small minority
followed Him. Most rejected his teachings and
remained in the well established, socially accepted
religions. In other words, they rejected the truth
so they could keep their religious traditions. Jesus
spoke the following words to those who did this:

> "… Full well ye reject the command-
> ment of God, that ye may keep your
> own tradition."   Mark 7:9

While Jesus was preaching, one listener who
began to comprehend this truth asked Jesus:

> "Lord, are there few that be saved?
> And he (Jesus) said unto them, Strive

to enter in at the strait gate: for many,
I say unto you, will seek to enter in,
and shall not be able." Luke 13:23-24

When Jesus taught his disciples to go out and
preach the gospel, he said:

"The harvest truly is plenteous, but
the labourers *are few;*" Matthew 9:37

In other words, most people are lost and need a
Savior, but few have the truth to go and tell
them.

Conclusion

Throughout this book, every Catholic doctrine
has violated God's Word. Yet millions of Catholics
ignore God's instructions and continue following
the traditions of men, claiming to be right because
they are in a religious majority. Jesus warns:

"… whosoever heareth these sayings
of mine, and doeth them, I will liken
him unto a wise man… And every
one that heareth these sayings of
mine, and doeth them not, shall be
likened unto *a foolish man…*"
                                    Matthew 7:24, 26

Does God consider you a wise or foolish person?
If you believe you can ignore God's commands

because you are in a religious majority, you need to read Matthew 7:24-26 again.

Jesus gives another warning to the majority who have disregarded God's Word and are counting on earning their salvation through good works:

> "Many will say to me in that day, Lord, Lord, have we not prophesied in thy name? and in thy name have cast out devils? and in thy name done *many wonderful works?* And then will I profess unto them, *I never knew you:* depart from me, ye that work iniquity."   Matthew 7:22-23

How is it that so many Catholics can call Jesus their Lord, yet totally disregard His instructions? Jesus asked that very same question in His Word:

> "And why call ye me, Lord, Lord, and do not the things which I say?"
>
> Luke 6:46

You can ignore this question now, but what will you say when Jesus asks you the same question in person when you die and stand before Him for judgment?

35

Reconciliation

A Catholic who is reconciled to God is simultaneously reconciled to the Catholic church, the Catechism asserts:

> "Forgiveness of sins brings reconciliation with God, but also with the Church." Pg. 367, #1462

Again, the Bible and the Catechism are at odds. God's Word does teach the necessity of being reconciled to God, but not to a church:

> "And, having made peace through the blood of his cross, by him to reconcile all things *unto himself;* by him…"
>
> Colossians 1:20

> "And all things are of God, who hath reconciled us *to himself* by Jesus Christ, and hath given to us the ministry of reconciliation;"
>
> 2 Corinthians 5:18

Paul, the Apostle, prayed that people would be reconciled to God, but never that they would be reconciled to the Catholic church:

> "Now then we are ambassadors for Christ, as though God did beseech you by us: we pray you in Christ's stead, ***be ye reconciled to God.***"
>
> 2 Corinthians 5:20

This same Paul preached:

> "And that he (Jesus) might reconcile both ***unto God*** in one body by the cross, having slain the enmity thereby:"
>
> Ephesians 2:16

Theme of the Bible

The theme of the entire Bible is man being reconciled to God through the shed blood of Jesus Christ. It is foreshadowed in the Old Testament and illustrated in the New Testament.

The heart of the Christian faith is the beautiful story of sinful man being reconciled to a holy and just God through the blood of Jesus Christ:

> "Therefore as by the offence of one (Adam) judgment came upon all men to condemnation; even so by the righteousness of one (Jesus) the free

> gift came upon all men unto ***justification*** of life." Romans 5:18

Being reconciled to God is Biblical, but being reconciled to the Catholic church is a tradition of men.

The Catechism threatens that if you are not reconciled to the Catholic church, you might not go to heaven. Where did they get the authority to create such a doctrine, since it is not found in the Bible?

Is this but another man-made doctrine designed to keep people in bondage to the Catholic church. While it sure appears to be, you must make the final decision for yourself.

Who will you be reconciled to?

Today, even though the Bible declares that our eternal destiny will be determined by whether or not we have been reconciled to God, millions of Catholics live in mortal fear of dying without being reconciled to the Catholic church, but have no fear of passing on without being reconciled to God.

If God really meant what He said in His Word, you, as a faithful Catholic, are making a mistake you will regret through all eternity.

Conclusion

Here are three additional questions for you to ponder:

1. If a person is already reconciled to the God of the universe, does it really matter if he or she has been reconciled to the Catholic church?

2. If your eternal destiny does rest upon being reconciled to a church, would God omit such vital information from His Word?

3. Why does Catholic doctrine once again directly contradict Biblical doctrine, and even the very words of Jesus Christ?

What about you? Are you more concerned about being reconciled to God, or to the Catholic church?

> "For if, when we were enemies, we were reconciled *to God* by the death of his Son, much more, being reconciled, we shall be saved by his life."
>
> Romans 5:10

36

Celibacy

"All the ordained ministers of the Latin Church, with the exception of permanent deacons, are normally chosen from among men of faith who live a celibate life and who intend to remain celibate 'for the sake of the kingdom of heaven'... Celibacy is a sign of this new life to the service of which the Church's minister is consecrated; accepted with a joyous heart celibacy radiantly proclaims the Reign of God."
Pg. 395, #1579

Is celibacy a sacrifice God requires of His servants, or is it another tradition of men? The Bible declares:

"Marriage is honourable *in all...*"
Hebrews 13:4

Does this include religious leaders, like priests and nuns? When God's Word lists the qualifications of bishops, who are religious leaders, we are told that:

> "A bishop then must be blameless, ***the husband of one wife...***"
>
> 1 Timothy 3:2

God has the same requirement for deacons:

> "Let the deacons be ***the husbands of one wife,*** ruling their children and their own houses well."
>
> 1 Timothy 3:12

From the beginning, it has always been God's plan that men should have wives. Shortly after creating Adam, the first man:

> "... the LORD God said, ***It is not good that the man should be alone;*** I will make him an help meet for him."
>
> Genesis 2:18

Not only does God express His approval of marriage, He delivers this powerful warning:

> "Now the Spirit speaketh expressly, that in the latter times some shall depart from the faith, giving heed to ***seducing spirits, and doctrines of devils;*** Speaking ***lies*** in hypocrisy; having their conscience seared with a hot iron; ***Forbidding to marry,*** and commanding to abstain from meats, which God hath created to be received

with thanksgiving of them which
believe and know the truth."

1 Timothy 4:1-3

Not only is celibacy not required by God, it is a
doctrine of demons. The Bible announces that
those who teach this doctrine are "giving heed to
seducing spirits, and doctrines of devils; Speaking
lies in hypocrisy;"

Please understand, these are not my words, they
are *God's Words.*

How tragic that priests and nuns around the
world are foregoing the pleasure of sharing their
lives with a spouse, believing that their sacrifice
pleases God, when in reality they are falling prey
to a powerful demonic scheme.

If only priests and nuns could learn that God
makes no such requirement... and that they are
being deceived by Satan. God has recorded all
these truths in His Word. If only they could see
and understand them.

A married pope?

Few Catholics realize that Peter, the "first pope,"
was a married man:

"But *Simon's wife's* mother lay sick of
a fever..."

Mark 1:30

This Simon is none other than the Apostle Peter. (See Matthew 4:18 and Matthew 10:2.)

Why this doctrine?

This Catholic doctrine, like all others we have discussed, directly opposes God's Word. One must wonder why Catholicism would teach that celibacy "radiantly proclaims the Reign of God," when the Lord has declared that this doctrine originated in hell.

Is it because the Catholic church does not want to pay the millions of dollars it would cost each year to support the families of priests and nuns?

Conclusion

Now that you know what the Bible teaches on this subject, you must decide whether you will believe the Word of God or the traditions of the Catholic church.

If you happen to be a priest or a nun, please ask yourself who your sacrifice is really pleasing:

> "Let thy fountain be blessed: and *rejoice with the wife of thy youth.*"
>
> Proverbs 5:18

37

Last Rites

The final doctrine we will review is also the last ritual many Catholics perform—viaticum, also known as the Last Rites:

> "As the sacrament of Christ's Passover the Eucharist should always be the last sacrament of the earthly journey, the 'viaticum' for 'passing over' to eternal life." Pg. 379, #1517

This ritual includes anointing the dying person:

> "If the sacrament of anointing of the sick is given to all who suffer from serious illness and infirmity, even more rightly is it given to those at the point of departing this life... The Anointing of the Sick completes our conformity to the death and Resurrection of Christ, just as Baptism began it." Pg. 381, #1523

The belief that this anointing "completes our conformity to the death and Resurrection of Christ" is another tradition of men the Scriptures say nothing about.

More bondage

Since this ritual can only be performed by a priest or other Catholic leader, it keeps members in bondage to the Catholic religion right up until the moment of their death:

> "Only priests (bishops and presbyters) are ministers of the Anointing of the Sick." Pg. 379, #1516

The Catechism also teaches that the Last Rites are the "seed of eternal life":

> "In addition to the Anointing of the Sick, the Church offers those who are about to leave this life the Eucharist as viaticum. Communion in the body and blood of Christ, received at this moment of 'passing over' to the Father, has particular significance and importance. It is the seed of eternal life and the power of resurrection…" Pg. 381, #1524

But the Bible disagrees, declaring that this ritual is neither the "seed of eternal life" nor the "power of resurrection." These are man-made doctrines that God neither initiated nor endorsed.

This act is nothing more than one final earthly good work, which the Bible proclaims to be useless:

> "… that I may win Christ. And be

found in him, ***not having mine own righteousness,*** which is of the law, but that which is through the faith of Christ, the righteousness which is of God ***by faith:"*** Philippians 3:8-9

Here are a few more man-made rules associated with this ritual:

"If a sick person who received this anointing recovers his health, he can in the case of another grave illness receive this sacrament again. If during the same illness the person's condition becomes more serious, the sacrament may be repeated. It is fitting to receive the Anointing just prior to a serious operation. The same holds true for the elderly whose frailty becomes more pronounced." Pg. 379, 1515

Rules on top of more rules. Please remember, God never ordained ***any*** of them. Men created them all.

Conclusion

As you make your own decision on this doctrine, here are a few points to consider:

- This ritual is never taught in the Bible.
- Not one Bible character ever received the Last Rites, including Paul, who said:

> "For I am now ready to be offered,
> and the time of my departure is at
> hand. I have fought a good fight, I
> have finished my course, I have kept
> the faith:"   2 Timothy 4:6-7

- Not one Bible character ever administered
  the Last Rites.

This doctrine overflows with commandments of
men. Will you place your faith and trust in these
man-made rules and regulations, or in Jesus
Christ?

Remember, Jesus warned:

> "But in vain they do worship me,
> teaching for doctrines the command-
> ments of men."   Matthew 15:9

Appendix 1

Confusion

After studying the 1994 Catechism, one cannot help but notice several major differences between Catholic doctrine and the Bible.

First and foremost is that both consistently teach conflicting doctrines. The Catechism's claim that the Bible and Catholic tradition work together to bring about the salvation of souls is simply not true.

Secondly, the Catechism contains an endless list of complicated and often confusing rules which all Catholics must follow to please their church.

The Bible, on the other hand, is simple, straightforward, consistent and easy to understand. Here is an example.

Who will go to heaven?

The Bible could not be any more explicit on the subject of eternal destiny, which is to be expected from God on such an important topic:

> "He that ***believeth*** on the Son ***hath***
> everlasting life: and he that ***believeth***
> ***not*** the Son ***shall not*** see life; but the
> wrath of God abideth on him."
>
> John 3:36

Here's another example. Jesus Himself preached:

> "He that heareth my word, and
> ***believeth on him that sent me, hath***
> ***everlasting life,*** and shall not come
> into condemnation; but is passed
> from death unto life."   John 5:24

That is very easy to understand. Now let's see
what the Catechism says on the same subject.
Here is an exact quote:

> "By virtue of our apostolic authority, we define
> the following: According to the general dis-
> position of God, the souls of all the saints…
> and other faithful who died after receiving
> Christ's holy Baptism (provided they were not
> in need of purification when they died,… or, if
> they then did need or will need some purifi-
> cation, when they have been purified after
> death,…) already before they take up their
> bodies again and before the general judgment-
> and this since the Ascension of our Lord and
> Savior Jesus Christ into heaven—have been, are
> and will be in heaven, in the heavenly

Kingdom and celestial paradise with Christ, joined to the company of the holy angels. Since the Passion and death of our Lord Jesus Christ, these souls have seen and do see the divine essence with an intuitive vision, and even face to face, without mediation of any creature." Pg. 267, #1023

Who could possibly understand that?

Why is such a simple Bible concept made so confusing? Surely God wants everyone to understand how to get to heaven. Would a truly loving God make the rules for reaching heaven so complex that nobody could understand them?

Consider also the following verse of Scripture:

> "For God is ***not the author of confusion,*** but of peace, as in all churches of the saints."   1 Corinthians 14:33

If God is not the author of this confusing list of Catholic rules, then who is?

Don't be deceived

The Bible even warns us about being deceived by those who complicate the simple things of Christ:

> "But I fear, lest by any means, as the serpent beguiled Eve through his subtility, so your minds should be

corrupted from the *simplicity* that is
in Christ."   2 Corinthians 11:3

Could God be attempting to warn you about the
Catholic church? God made His Word simple
because He is:

"… not willing that any should perish,
but that all should come to repentance."   2 Peter 3:9

God wants you in heaven. That's why He keeps
His Word simple.

Conclusion

God does not want you to be confused. If the
Catechism and Catholic doctrine have ever left
you feeling confused, perhaps you should begin
putting your trust in God's Word:

"In thee, O LORD, do I put my trust:
let me never be put to confusion."
                              Psalm 71:1

Appendix 2

An Invitation

This book was not written to attack or criticize Catholic people. Having been born and raised as a Roman Catholic, I understand how average Catholics think and feel about their religion.

Two factors motivated the writing of this book. First, I want you to know that your religion is not Biblical. It is a religion comprised of traditions of men which violate scripture at every turn.

Secondly, I would love for you to experience the freedom and peace I found when I broke free from the bondage of the Catholic church by placing my hope for salvation in Jesus Christ alone.

Tens of thousands of other former Catholics have experienced this same freedom and peace.

As I mentioned, I was raised a Roman Catholic. I was baptized shortly after birth. I received my First Communion and Confirmation. During grade school, I attended weekly religious instruction classes and attended Mass each Sunday. I confessed my sins to a priest and regularly received Communion.

At age 18, I enlisted in the United States Navy, leaving home and the Catholic church behind. While in the military, a friend invited me to a Baptist church. Though somewhat resistant, I agreed to try it once.

That first service was one I will never forget. When the pastor preached, he seemed to be talking straight at me. He concluded his sermon by inviting those who wanted to repent of their sins and be saved to come up front.

My heart began pounding like a jackhammer. I knew something powerful was going on but I felt frozen in my seat.

The pastor ended the service that morning with these words, "I believe that someone said no to Jesus Christ today. I pray you won't die before you have another opportunity to receive Him, or you will spend eternity separated from God." I knew he was talking to me.

Within seconds, the pounding stopped. It was so real. God had spoken to me—and I had said no:

> "Behold, I stand at the door, and knock: if any man hear my voice, and open the door, I will come in to him, and will sup with him, and he with me."   Revelation 3:20

A couple of days later the same friend invited me to church again. I could hardly wait. Again, the pastor preached and as his sermon came to a close the pounding in my chest resumed. When the pastor gave the invitation, I bolted from my seat.

A young man opened his Bible and explained how I could receive the gift of eternal life. I learned from God's Word that we are all sinners in need of a Savior, and that Jesus Christ paid the full price for all our sins on the cross.

This young man showed me from the Bible how I could be saved right then by repenting of my sins and asking Jesus Christ to come into my heart to be my personal Lord and Savior.

In my own words, I admitted to God that I was a sinner who deserved hell, and I asked Jesus Christ to come into my heart and save me.

I cannot explain the feeling, but it was like a thousand pound weight was hoisted off my shoulders. Instantly, I knew I had been set free. I knew that Jesus had come into my heart and made me a brand new person. A lifetime of good works could never accomplish the miracle that took place in those few moments.

It has been over twenty five years since that day, and although I have failed the Lord many times, He has never failed me or left me. He is more real and more precious to me today than ever. I would not trade places with anyone or give up my relationship with Jesus for anything this world has to offer.

Precious Roman Catholic, that same freedom and joy is available to you. You can receive Jesus Christ as your Savior right now. You have heard the truth and now you can be made free:

> "And ye shall know the truth, and the truth shall make you free." John 8:32

The wonderful goodness of God is leading you to repentance and salvation:

> "Or despisest thou the riches of his goodness and forbearance and long-suffering; not knowing that the *goodness of God leadeth thee to repentance?*" Romans 2:4

God wants you to be saved today:

> "... behold, *now* is the accepted time;

> behold, ***now is the day of salvation.***"
> 2 Corinthians 6:2

If you would like to become a child of God, bow your head and talk to God from your heart. In your own words, pray something like this:

> "Dear Jesus, I admit that I'm a sinner. I repent of all my sins and I ask you to come into my heart and save me.
>
> I repent of trusting in a false religion that demands good works for salvation. I now see that You paid the full price for all my sins on the cross. I reject the teachings of Catholicism and I place my trust in you alone.
>
> From now on Your Word will be the final authority in my life, not the traditions of the Catholic church.
>
> Thank you, Lord, for saving me and for giving me the gift of eternal life. In Jesus' name, Amen."

If you just prayed a prayer similar to this one and really meant it, then you were just born into God's family:

> "But as many as received him, to them gave he power to become the sons of

God, even to them that believe on his
name:"   John 1:12

My friend, this entire book was written so you
could hear and be convinced by God of the truth
of this message. If you have not already done so,
please receive the gift of eternal life. Only then
will you experience the joy and peace of knowing
your sins are forgiven.

My prayer is twofold:

• First, that you will begin a personal relationship
with God through faith alone in Jesus Christ.

• Secondly, that you will be set free from the
bondage of the Catholic church.

This book was not written to criticize you, but to
lead you to these wonderful truths. May God
bless you as you begin your new life in Him:

"Every good gift and every perfect gift
is from above, and cometh down from
the Father of lights, with whom is no
variableness, neither shadow of turn-
ing."   James 1:17

Appendix 3

God's Plea

Hopefully, you have just asked Jesus to come into your heart and have been born again scripturally. If so, according to the Bible, one of your first acts should be to come out of the Catholic church:

> "... Come out of her, my people, that ye be not partakers of her sins, and that ye receive not of her plagues."
>
> Revelation 18:4

Many Roman Catholics claim to be born again Christians, yet contend that God wants them to remain in the Catholic church. However, Scripture declares that God does not want His children worshipping Him in a false, idolatrous religion. On the contrary, He says come out and stay out:

> "Stand fast therefore in the liberty wherewith Christ hath made us free, and *be not entangled again with the yoke of bondage.*"   Galatians 5:1

209

Many other verses teach us the same lesson:

> "Be ye not unequally yoked together with unbelievers: for what fellowship hath righteousness with unrighteousness? and what communion hath light with darkness?   2 Corinthians 6:14

Should you worship with those who deny God's Word?

> "And if any man obey not our word by this epistle, note that man, **and have no company with him,** that he may be ashamed."
>
> 2 Thessalonians 3:14

Many Catholics give various excuses for remaining in the Catholic church, but good intentions do not impress God when they cause you to disobey His Word. More than anything, God wants obedience:

> "Thou shalt therefore **obey the voice of the LORD** thy God, and do his commandments and his statutes..."
>
> Deuteronomy 27:10

> "Whether it be good, or whether it be evil, **we will obey the voice of the LORD our God..."**   Jeremiah 42:6

Obedience or sacrifice?

Sometimes Catholics remain in the church, insisting that they are sacrificing their personal desires for the good of others. But God would rather have obedience than sacrifice:

> "… Hath the LORD as great delight in burnt offerings and sacrifices, as in obeying the voice of the LORD? Behold, *to obey is better than sacrifice…"* 1 Samuel 15:22

Why won't people come out?

Despite God's clear instructions in His Word, some people still refuse to leave the Catholic church. There are two possible reasons why:

1. They are saved but honestly don't know that God wants them to leave the church.

2. They think they are saved but aren't, because in their heart their hope for salvation is still in the Catholic church, and they are afraid to leave.

Only you can tell which category you fit in because no one else knows your heart.

Was he really converted?

I remember talking with a Catholic young man who willingly admitted his lost condition and his need to trust Christ as Savior. He prayed and asked Jesus to come into his heart. He had no problem with that.

Then I told him he needed to leave the Catholic church. He recoiled and blurted out, "Oh, I could **never** leave the Catholic church!"

"Why not?" I asked.

He explained that he had been born and raised in the Catholic church and that the church was necessary for salvation. Whether this young man understood it or not, his hope for eternal life was in the Catholic church, not in Jesus Christ.

Like him, many Catholics today claim to be born again, yet refuse to obey God. Certainly, no one can judge another man's salvation, but the Bible does reveal that those who trust in traditions of men will be bitterly disappointed on Judgment Day:

> "Thus saith the LORD; Cursed be the man that trusteth in man, and maketh flesh his arm, and whose heart departeth from the LORD."
>
> Jeremiah 17:5

If you are a Catholic who refuses to come out of Catholicism, you are, at best, a Christian living in disobedience to God, and, at worst, an unsaved person deceived into thinking you are a Christian:

> "And ***have no fellowship*** with the unfruitful works of darkness, but rather reprove them." Ephesians 5:11

If you really want to please God, you must obey Him and leave this system that denies His truths.

No fear

Another reason people don't leave the Catholic church is fear. The church has instilled in them the belief that salvation is available only through the Catholic church! I remember being taught as a child that it was a mortal sin to attend any other religious service while it was in progress.

However, God's Word assures those who have been born again that they need not fear:

> "For God hath not given us the spirit of fear; but of power, and of love, and of a sound mind." 2 Timothy 1:7

You need not fear leaving the Roman Catholic church. Jesus Christ will take good care of you.

No more idols

To help you be set free from the power of this false church, it is important that you remove from your home anything associated with it, like statues, rosary beads, Catechisms, prayer books, etc. These are all idolatrous items, and God hates idolatry:

> "Wherefore, my dearly beloved, *flee from idolatry.*" 1 Corinthians 10:14

The Apostle Paul plainly states that those who practice idolatry will not go to heaven. (See Galatians 5:19-21.)

The best way to dispose of these idolatrous items is to burn them (see Acts 19:19).

"I'll reach them from within"

Another excuse people use to avoid leaving the Catholic church is that they want to win those still in the church from within.

But the truth is, the best way to win others is to obey God so you can have His power in your life. It doesn't make sense to disobey God to do His work better. If God instructs you to come out of the Catholic church, then you should obey Him.

A converted priest

Several years ago, a Catholic priest who learned that his church was in error asked Jesus to come into his heart and save him.

In obedience to God, he left the Catholic church.

But every Sunday morning he drove back to his old church and sat in his car in the parking lot. After Mass, as former parishioners walked by and recognized him, they'd say something like, "Hey, Father, we heard you left the church. What happened to you?"

He'd reply, "Yes, I did leave because something exciting happened. Hop in the car and I'll tell you all about it." Using that method, he led over half his former congregation to true salvation in Jesus Christ.

Conclusion

So, my friend, the choice is yours. If you are now a true Christian, you know what God wants you to do. The question is, "Will you obey Him?"

> "Wherefore ***come out from among them,*** and be ye separate, saith the Lord, and touch not the unclean thing; and I will receive you,"
>
> 2 Corinthians 6:17

Appendix 4

Liberty or Bondage?

One theme has run throughout each chapter of this book. It is the major difference between Catholicism and true Christianity:

- **Catholicism brings people into bondage.**

- **Jesus Christ sets people free.**

You may have noticed that every doctrine of Catholicism brings members into bondage to the Catholic church. You need the church to be saved. You need the church to receive forgiveness for your sins. You need the church for *everything!*

By design, you are in bondage to the Catholic church from shortly after birth at baptism until the moment of your death when you receive the Last Rites.

But the Bible declares that Jesus died to set you free from that bondage:

"Because the creature itself also shall

217

be delivered from the bondage of corruption into the glorious liberty of the children of God."   Romans 8:21

Paul preached:

"For ye have not received the spirit of bondage again to fear; but ye have received the Spirit of adoption, whereby we cry, Abba, Father."

Romans 8:15

Christ sets people free. Religion brings them into bondage:

"… because of false brethren unawares brought in, who came in privily to spy out our liberty which we have in Christ Jesus, *that they might bring us into bondage:"*   Galatians 2:4

Don't be deceived! Religion promises liberty, but *always* delivers bondage:

"While they promise them liberty, they themselves are the servants of corruption: for of whom a man is overcome, of the same is he brought in bondage."   2 Peter 2:19

God's Word urges true Christians to stand fast in the liberty that only Christ can provide:

> "Stand fast therefore in the liberty wherewith Christ hath made us free, and be not entangled again with the yoke of bondage."   Galatians 5:1

The Apostle Paul knew about this liberty, and warned fellow Christians not to misuse it:

> "For, brethren, **ye have been called unto liberty;** only use not liberty for an occasion to the flesh, but by love serve one another."   Galatians 5:13

God doesn't want you toiling in bondage to a religion. He wants you to enjoy real liberty:

> "Now the Lord is that Spirit: and where the Spirit of the Lord is, there is **liberty.**"   2 Corinthians 3:17

> "And I will walk at **liberty:** for I seek thy precepts."   Psalm 119:45

Set free

As a former Roman Catholic, I know what this bondage is all about. Throughout my youth, I was taught Catholic rules and regulations, and I lived in fear of what would happen if I didn't obey them.

One of the greatest joys I experienced when I

asked Jesus into my heart was the liberty I found in Christ. The chains of bondage were broken off. Its power over me was lifted and I was set free.

Which will it be for you?

You can be delivered from the bondage of the Catholic church, and experience this same liberty. Jesus already did the work to set you free:

> "And deliver them who through fear of death were all their lifetime subject to bondage."   Hebrews 2:15

Paul discusses the same subject again:

> "Even so we, when we were children, were in bondage under the elements of the world: But when the fulness of the time was come, God sent forth his Son... To redeem them that were under the law, that we might receive the adoption of sons..."
>
> Galatians 4:3-5

Love or hate?

Paul follows these remarks with this statement:

> "Am I therefore become your enemy, because I tell you the truth?"
>
> Galatians 4:16

In closing, I ask you the same question. Am I your enemy because I have told you the truth? Some will certainly suggest that I am against Catholics. I am not!

On the contrary, I have presented here the one and only message that can spare Catholics (and all people) from an eternity in the lake of fire. That's not hate, that's love.

I want all Catholics to receive the gift of eternal life. I want you to be set free from a religion that enslaves you. That's not hate, that's love.

I want you to experience the joy and peace that only Jesus Christ can give. That's not being an enemy... that's being a friend.

Your real enemy

You do have an enemy, though. His name is Satan. He hates you and wants you to burn in hell forever:

> "Be sober, be vigilant; because your adversary the devil, as a roaring lion, walketh about, *seeking whom he may devour:*" 1 Peter 5:8

The devil knows that to devour you he must keep you from obeying God's Word.

Here's his plan:

First, he creates a religion, complete with all the religious trappings to make it appear authentic.

Next, he formulates unbiblical doctrines that members must perform. People become so busy obeying these rules they never find Christ.

Another earmark of Satan's religions is the denigrating of Jesus Christ. The devil hates Jesus and knows that He is the only way to heaven (John 14:6). Therefore, Satan will do everything He can to keep people's eyes off Christ.

Unfortunately, this plan has been working for centuries. Don't underestimate Satan. He is a master deceiver. (See Revelation 12:9.)

Please don't let the devil deceive you any longer. *He* is your real enemy and he is using a religion to keep you away from Jesus Christ. Please don't let him keep you away any longer.

Turn to Jesus today. He is waiting to set you free. God bless you as you experience true salvation in Jesus Christ:

> "Trust in the LORD with all thine heart; and lean not unto thine own understanding. In all thy ways acknowledge him, and he shall direct thy paths."   Proverbs 3:5-6

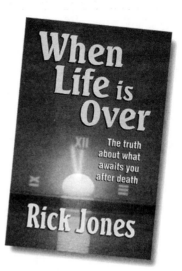
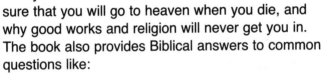